Author, playwright, translator, theater and film director Roger Pulvers received his MA in Russian Studies at Harvard Graduate School and did post-graduate work at Warsaw University in Poland before arriving in Japan in the summer of 1967. He has published more than fifty books in Japanese and English, including novels such as *The Death of Urashima Taro*, *General Yamashita's Treasure*, *Star Sand*, *Liv*, *The Dream of Lafcadio Hearn* and *Peaceful Circumstances*.

In 2017 the feature film of *Star Sand*, written and directed by him, had wide release throughout Japan and screened on prime-time Japanese television. He is also the author of two memoirs: *My Japan: a Cultural Memoir* and *The Unmaking of an American*, both published by Balestier Press.

Roger has worked extensively in radio, film and television. He was assistant to director Oshima Nagisa on the film "Merry Christmas, Mr. Lawrence" and co-wrote the script for "Ashita e no Yuigon" (Best Wishes for Tomorrow), for which he won the Crystal Simorgh Prize for Best Script at the 27th Fajr International Film Festival in Tehran.

Roger received the prestigious Miyazawa Kenji Prize in 2008 and the Noma Award for the Translation of Japanese Literature in 2013; in 2018, Japan's highest honor, the Order of the Rising Sun; and in 2019, the Order of Australia. Over the past fifty years he has translated prose, drama and poetry from Japanese, Russian and Polish, and his plays have been widely performed in Australia, Japan and the United States.

POEMS 2020

Translation from
Russian, Polish and Japanese
Notes and Commentary by

ROGER PULVERS

BALESTIER PRESS
LONDON · SINGAPORE

Balestier Press
Centurion House, London TW18 4AX
www.balestier.com

Poems 2020: Translation from Russian, Polish and Japanese, Notes and Commentary
Copyright © Roger Pulvers, 2021

Poems by Terayama Shuji used by permission.

All Japanese names are given in Japanese order with surname before given name.

A CIP catalogue record for this book is available from the British Library.

ISBN 978 1 913891 15 2

Cover illustration by Lucy Pulvers

CONTENTS

Poems from Polish by Author

Poems from Japanese by Author

Introduction

The year 2020 was the year the world turned inward.

The people of the world suddenly found themselves faced with the same challenge. COVID-19 was, in that sense, even more unifying than war. No single war has ever been fought by all nations. When I was in the Cook Islands in 1982 for the filming of "Merry Christmas, Mr. Lawrence," an old man told me that he hadn't known there was a war on in the Pacific until after it was over. "I did see one big ship on the horizon," he said, "but I didn't know it was a warship." I don't think the same could be said for COVID-19.

From March until December 2020 I translated poems from the three languages that I happen to know and recorded readings on the YouTube channel "Roger Pulvers Reads." I made these recordings every three days until I had done one hundred of them. It was wonderful to receive responses from people around the world. One came from a grandchild of Konstanty Ildefons Gałczyński. As I mention in the commentary on him, she and Gałczyński's four other grandchildren all settled in Australia.

I have added biographical commentary, as many readers may be unfamiliar with some of the poets, as well as notes to explain references to places, customs, etc.

The poets appearing here describe not only affairs of the heart but also upheaval and revolution, exile and betrayal, and encounters and events that are often brimming with hilarity and wit, proving without a doubt that poetry is the lifeblood of every nation.

May these poems bring you a bit of inspiration, a good deal of consolation and much much joy. These are poems I love. I hope you love them too.

Roger Pulvers
Sydney 2021

Poems from Russian

NIKOLAI GUMILEV (1886-1921) was considered the leader of the Acmeist group of poets that prominently included Osip Mandelstam and Anna Akhmatova. The group took its name from the Greek word denoting "the height, the very best," emphasizing a formality of technique and clarity of expression, where words are considered material in the creation of a craft. The Acmeists were enamored of the ancient world, with its symmetry and classic beauty. (If some of the Acmeists, notably Mandelstam, created verse whose meaning was not readily accessible, they would argue that they were striving for precision, not simplicity.) Gumilev was also a brilliant translator and critic.

Gumilev (pronounced Goo-mil-YOV) traveled extensively throughout Africa and Europe, fought in World War I and was awarded two St. George Crosses, about which his wife, poet Anna Akhmatova, wrote these lines to their son Lev:

> *They bestowed on your father*
> *A little white cross*

Gumilev and Akhmatova married in 1910, and Lev was born two years later. But the marriage of two of Russia's greatest poets was by no means a happy one and did not last long. He served in France in the Russian Expeditionary Force, returning to St. Petersburg, then called Petrograd, in April 1918 after landing in Murmansk on a British ship. (In London he had met the young Aldous Huxley and other cultural figures.)

He and Akhmatova officially divorced that year. It was Akhmatova who asked him, bluntly, for the divorce. Both promptly remarried, Gumilev to Anna Engelhardt, whose father, also called Nikolai, was a well-known author and journalist and whose mother had been married to Konstantin Balmont (see page 64). Some people called Gumilev's new wife "Anna II." She was arrested in the 1930s and died with her and Gumilev's daughter during the siege of Leningrad.

(The city will be referred to as St. Petersburg unless a specific event or series of events indicates one of its other names is more appropriate.)

As for Gumilev himself, he was arrested in August 1921 on trumped up charges for being part of the so-called pro-monarchy Tagantsev Conspiracy, which, in any case, was a fabrication of the Cheka, the secret police organization of the new Bolshevik state.

Gumilev fully expected that he would be exonerated, if only because of his immense reputation. After all, Nicholas I had pardoned Pushkin. Gorky interceded with Lenin on Gumilev's behalf, but Lenin deferred to Felix Dzerzhinsky, the ruthless director of the Cheka. Dzerzhinsky is reported as saying that he wasn't going to free a poet "and still shoot the others."

On 26 August 1921 Gumilev was shot—along with sixty-one others, including Vladimir Tagantsev, who was a member of the Russian Academy of Sciences and the son of a senator in the old regime—and buried in the Kovalesky Forest near St. Petersburg. It is estimated that approximately 4,500 victims of the Red Terror are buried there.

As Akhmatova was later to write …

The soil of Russia
Loves, just loves blood

THE TRAM THAT LOST ITS WAY
NIKOLAI GUMILEV

for Numano Kyoko and Numano Mitsuyoshi

I was walking on a strange and unfamiliar street
When a crow cawed out of the blue.
I heard the strains of a lute and distant thunder.
A tram flew by right under my nose.

It's a mystery to me how I managed
To hop onto its running board.
The tram even left behind a trail of fire
In the air of that sunlit day.

It tore through that air, a dark winged storm
Losing its way in the chasm of time …
Stop this tram, conductor!
Stop it this very instant!

Not in time … we'd gone around a wall
And were speeding through a thicket of pine.
We roared over three bridges
Across the Neva, across the Nile, the Seine.

A poor old beggar tossed us a curious glance
As we flashed under a window frame
Naturally the very same man
Who died a year ago in Beirut.

Where am I? My heart, alarmed
Beat out a faint answer:
"Can you see that station where they sell
Tickets to the India of the Mind?"

There's a shop sign … it says "Greens"
In letters dripping with blood.
On sale, I know, are not cabbages or swedes
But the severed heads of the dead.

The executioner slices off my head too
In his red shirt and udder face.
It sits at the very bottom of a slippery box
Under all the other heads.

There's a house with three windows on a little street
A gray lawn and a fence of planks.
Stop this tram, conductor!
Stop it this very instant!

You lived and sang here, dear Mashenka
You wove me a rug, me, your fiancé.
Where are your voice and body now?
Could it be that you are dead?

How you moaned in your sitting room
Whilst I, in my powdered plaits, went off

To introduce myself to the Empress
Never to set eyes on you again.

It's clear to me now: Our freedom
Is a light shining only from that place
Where people and shadows stand at the entrance
To a planetary zoo.

Without warning a familiar sweet breeze
And the iron-gloved hand of a horseman
And two hooves of his horse
Fly at me from beyond the bridge.

St. Isaac's, bastion of Orthodox faith
Is etched into the dome of the sky.
I will conduct an occasional service for Mashenka
And a memorial service for myself.

My heart is steeped in eternal gloom.
Breathing is hard and life a pain …
Mashenka, I never so much as imagined
That I could love and mourn like this.

"The Tram That Lost Its Way," published in 1921, is a prophetic poem foreshadowing
the troubles and terrors brought by the revolution, inspired in its otherworldliness,
in part, by Yevgeny Zamyatin's 1918 very short story "The Dragon," in which a soldier
is transformed into a beast and kills a man who has "the mug of an intellectual." The

story ends with the monster "grinding its teeth and soaring into the unknown, away from the world of men, a tram."

The image of the severed heads on sale at the greengrocer's in place of cabbages and swedes in Gumilev's poem is a mark of those terrors, as is the tram itself, which, like a revolution, is difficult to brake once set in motion.

The three rivers mentioned in the poem—the Neva, the Seine and the Nile—had all seen violent upheavals, revolutions in the case of the first two and an exodus of a nation of people in the case of the third. There are also references to the old world of faith and royalty discarded by the new regime as relics of evil.

THE GIRAFFE
NIKOLAI GUMILEV

Today I see you're more wistful than usual
With skinny arms wrapped round your knees
Sh! … Far, far away an exquisite giraffe
Is roaming over Lake Chad

With an upright ease and the gift of grace
And a magical pattern adorning its skin
That only the moon would dare emulate
It springs and scatters on boundless waters

It looks from afar like the colorful sails on a ship
And it soars as it runs with the joy of a bird in flight
There are many miracles to be seen on this Earth …
A giraffe at sunset in the guise of a sculpted sail

I know cheerful tales of curious countries
Of mysterious maidens and young rulers' passions
You've breathed in dense fog for far too long
To wish for faith in anything but rain

So let me tell you the story of a tropical garden
Of upright palms and grassland's singular scent …
Are you weeping? Sh! … Far, far away an exquisite giraffe
Is roaming over Lake Chad

In 1909 Gumilev wrote to the great symbolist poet Innokenty Annensky (whom Akhmatova had called "her teacher") that he considered the "Lake Chad" cycle of poems, in which "The Giraffe" was included, "my favorite works." These poems, published in 1908, are the first in Russian to be set in Africa, where he had visited the previous year. He was an inveterate traveler who for much of his adult life spent more time away from Russia than within its borders.

The scattered light of the giraffe's body as it sails over the water is painterly in an impressionistic manner. Perhaps it was only such images of a land far away from Russia that could give him the consolation unobtainable at home. Gumilev wrote many poems about such far-flung places, including Venice, Rome, Constantinople, Addis Ababa, Liberia and Niger.

BORIS PASTERNAK (1890-1960) is more well known outside Russia as a novelist than a poet, thanks to the popularity of his drippy novel *Doctor Zhivago*, which prompted the committee of judges of the Nobel Prize for Literature to award it to him in 1958. (He, however, felt compelled to decline the prize after being "counseled" by the Soviet government and, in fact, some of his colleagues that it wasn't in his interests to accept.) He was also a wonderful translator, primarily of work originally in German, English and Georgian. Pasternak was "rehabilitated" in stages beginning five years after his death, and in 1987 reinstated into the Union of Writers of the USSR, just before its collapse.

There is an overall sense of humility permeating Pasternak's poems. He is not the type to gush over his emotions. I would call his style dry and subtly controlled. Sometimes he is downright self-effacing, as in his famous poem "It is not Pretty to be Famous," where he advises one …

> *To plunge into the unknown*
> *And hide in it your steps*
> *As a place hides itself in a fog*
> *And everything is black as pitch*
>
> *Let others follow you step by step*
> *Along the road you take*
> *You must not distinguish*
> *Between victories and defeats*

Pasternak spent much time in Germany, where he first visited as a fifteen-year-old in 1906, returning to Marburg for university. After the revolution he committed himself to life in his homeland, rejecting emigration.

Much is made of the telephone call from Stalin in 1934. The wily dictator asked him whether he supported his friend Osip Mandelstam, who had been arrested mainly due to the poem Mandelstam had written about Stalin (see page 40). Pasternak hemmed and hawed; and Stalin hung up on him after admonishing him for not coming to the aid of a fellow poet.

NIGHT

BORIS PASTERNAK

The night doesn't drag its feet.
It ebbs, while the flyer
Departs for the clouds
Above a slumbering world.

He drowned in the fog
Vanished in his stream
A cross-stitch on fabric
A mark on a wash of white.

Beneath him lie the nighttime bars
The unfamiliar cities
The ugly barracks, the stokers
The stations and the trains.

The framed shadow of his wing
Falls fully on a cloud
As heavenly bodies wander
Huddled in a mass.

The Milky Way is rotating
Listing in a horrific way
As it heads precariously
Toward an unknown universe.

Land masses are burning
In limitless spaces.
Welders are not asleep
In their boiler rooms and basements.

A Venus or a Mars
Is peering at a poster
That announces a new farce
From under a Paris rooftop.

A long lovely way away
Someone's wide awake
Under the sheltered tiles
Of an ancient attic.

He observes the planet
As if the sky was turning
Toward the subject
Of his nighttime cares.

Don't sleep, don't sleep, just work
Don't interrupt your toil.
Don't sleep, fight off that slumber
Like a flyer … like a star.

Don't sleep, don't sleep, my artist
Do not give in to sleep.
You are the hostage of eternity.
You are a prisoner of time.

"Night," written in 1957, is Pasternak's call to the artist to remain vigilant whatever transpires "on the ground." It contrasts the world of the sky, through which a flyer in his plane—or a poet in his imagination—soars, to the down-to-earth world of barracks, boiler rooms and basements. Love and war, in the guise of Venus and Mars, make an appearance; while artists, in the realm they preside over, are both the "hostage of eternity" and the "prisoner of time." There is no escaping this wakeful role in a slumbering world.

It is quite possible that Pasternak was inspired here by René Clair's 1930 film, and France's first talkie, "Under the Roofs of Paris"; as well as by the flights of Antoine de Saint-Exupéry.

ANNA AKHMATOVA (1889-1966), a member of the Acmeist group, was a poet whose poems are striking and intimate, whether she is confronting a lover or lamenting the horrors of her country's history. The horror that touched her most deeply was the persecution and arrest of her son Lev and the eventual exile of her husband, Futurist poet and author Nikolai Punin, who died in 1953, at the age sixty-four, in a Siberian gulag in Vorkuta, a coal-mining town north of the Arctic Circle. Her son Lev, whose father was her first husband, Nikolai Gumilev, was imprisoned from 1949 until 1956.

Akhmatova managed to escape Leningrad during World War II, taking refuge in Uzbekistan, where she spent more than two years and wrote two of her most famous poems, "Poem without a Hero" and "Courage." In "Courage" she wrote ...

> *We will protect you, Russian speech*
> *Great Russian word*
> *We will carry you forward, free and pure*
> *Pass you unfettered to our grandchildren*
> *Forever!*

After the war Akhmatova returned to Leningrad. In her cycle titled "Requiem," dated 1 April 1957, she wrote of the seventeen months she spent "waiting in lines in front of a prison" where her son was incarcerated.

> *The woman behind me had blue eyes. She had of course never heard my name.*

The woman whispers in her ear ("there everyone speaks in whispers") ...

> *"Can you really describe this?"*
> *And I said:*

"I can"
*Then something resembling a smile flitted across what had
    once resembled her face.*

Once back home after the war, Akhmatova was subjected to an onslaught of insults and accusations from official circles. Politburo member and chief of cultural affairs Andrei Zhdanov called her "part-nun, part-slut," and she was expelled from the Writers Union. Her works began to gradually reappear in the late 1950s. In 1965 she was awarded an honorary doctorate by Oxford University.

THE MUSE
ANNA AKHMATOVA

When at night I wait for her arrival
Life, it seems, is hanging by a thread
What are honors, what's youth … what is freedom
Before this lovely guest with flute in hand?

So she entered. And tossing aside her mantle
She looked at me with a piercing gaze
I ask her, "Was it you who dictated to Dante
The pages of Hell?" And she answers, "It was"

In "The Muse" Akhmatova reveals how, from where and from when inspiration appears—across borders of space and time. The "lovely guest" is Euterpe, one of the Muses, who presides over music and is historically depicted with a flute or pipes in her hand. Akhmatova knew her statue in Pavlovsk Park in St. Petersburg.

In "The Muse" poetry reigns over honors, youth and, even, freedom.

I HAVE LEARNED TO LIVE SIMPLY AND WISELY
ANNA AKHMATOVA

I have learned to live simply and wisely

To look to the sky when praying to God

Roaming and wandering the late afternoons

To drain away my needless anxieties

When burdock leaves are rustling in the ravine

And a yellow-red bundle of rowan berries droops down

I put joyous lines to paper

About mortal life … mortal and lovely

I come home. My fluffy cat

Licks my palm with ingratiating purrs

As the light burns brightly

On the tower of the sawmill by the lake

The only thing breaking the silence now and then

Is the cry of the stork descending to the roof

So it may be that I'll not even hear you

If you happen to be knocking on my door

"I Have Learned to Live Simply and Wisely" was written in 1912, the year in which Lev was born and Akhmatova's relationship with Gumilev was irretrievably on the rocks. They did not live together for much of their marriage. He loved travel to distant places more than intimate commitments at home; and she had affairs, famously with Amedeo Modigliani, who did sixteen drawings of her, one in the nude.

I'VE NO NEED FOR BATTLE EPICS

ANNA AKHMATOVA

I've no need for battle epics
Or the charms of elegiac fanfares
If you ask me, everything in a poem
Should be unsettled … out of place

If you only knew the kind of dregs
From which poems unashamedly grow
Like the yellow dandelions by the fence
Like burdock flowers, like saltbush

A shout in anger, the odor of fresh tar
A baffling mold on a wall …
And already the poem is impassioned and touching
To give us both pleasure and joy

"I've No Need for Battle Epics" beautifully illustrates the gestures, objects and images that can inspire poetry. Akhmatova is going against the grain of lofty inspiration, as well as ignoring the Soviet ukases to produce epic adulation.

THE GUEST
ANNA AKHMATOVA

It's all happened before ...
The fine blizzard's snow
Beating on the windows of my dining room.
I'm the same woman I was too
When a man came to see me.

I asked him, "What do you want?"
He said, "To join you in Hell."
"Ah," I laughed, "you're divining us both
Misery and misfortune."

But he raised a cold hand
Brushing against the flowers.
"Tell me," he said, "how others kiss you
And tell me how you kiss them back."

His colorless eyes
Fixed on my ring
And not a muscle moved
In his serenely wicked face.

Oh I know that his pleasure and bliss
Come from his rapt impassioned awareness

That there's nothing he's in need of
And nothing I can possibly refuse him.

"The Guest" was written in 1914, when Akhmatova was twenty-five. This guest remains intriguingly anonymous. Was he conjured up to make Gumilev jealous? After all, the ring on her finger is the one he gave her. Yet he had lost passion for her early in the marriage and, in any case, had spent 1913 largely in Africa, so it's not him.

CREATIVITY
ANNA AKHMATOVA

This is how it happens: a kind of listlessness
And the incessant striking of the clock in my ears.
Claps of thunder fade into the distance
And I imagine that I hear
The moaning and complaining
Of unidentified captive voices.
Some secret circle closes in around me.
And yet a single triumphant sound
Rises out of this chasm
The sound of whispering and ringing.
Surrounding it is an irreplaceable silence
So you can listen to the grass growing in the woods
And hear the evil goblin with his knapsack
Roaming over the earth....
And, look, the words can now be heard
With little bells calling out light rhymes.
It's then that I begin to understand
And the lines, simply dictated
Fall onto the pages of my snow-white pad.

Again Akhmatova turns to the creative process with its "whispering and ringing." The words seem to come to her, using her as a medium for them to turn from sounds to lines that are "simply dictated." "Creativity" was written in 1936 as part of a cycle titled "Secrets of the Trade." The key to the secret may lie in her use, close together, of "listen," "hear" and "look."

FROM "NORTHERN ELEGIES"
ANNA AKHMATOVA

There are three epochs to reminiscences
And the first is like a day gone by
The soul is below their blessed arch
The body delights in their shadows' bliss
Tears flow, laughter has not yet died out
The stain of ink remains unwiped on the table
And like a seal on the heart, a kiss
Single, parting, unforgettable …
But this doesn't last long

Now the arch above the head is gone, and somewhere
In a deaf suburb there's a solitary house
Where the winters are cold and the summers hot
Where there are spiders and sheets of dust
Where letters, like old flames, smolder
And portraits change in the stealth of night
Where people walk as if to a grave
And, having returned, wash their hands with soap
Shake off a fleeting little tear
From tired lids and heave a heavy sigh

But the clock ticks, one spring turns
Into another, the sky pales pink
The names of cities change
And soon witnesses to events are gone
There's no one to cry with, no one to reminisce with
Slowly the shadows leave us
Shadows which we call upon no longer
Shadows whose return would terrify us
And we wake to find we cannot even remember
The way to that solitary house
And choking with shame and anger
We rush there but, as it happens in dreams
Nothing is the same … people, objects, walls
And no one knows us there … we're strangers
We were in the wrong place … oh my God!
Then comes the bitterer misery

We become aware that there's no more room
For that past in the borders of our life
That past is nearly as alien to us
As it is to our neighbor across the hall
We know we would not recognize those who died
And those with whom God has parted us
Have done beautifully without us … and even
All's for the better

This is No. 4 in the cycle. It was written when Akhmatova returned home after World War II. Once again, due to political exigencies, "the names of cities change." She had lived in a city that had been known as St. Petersburg (and was the capital at the time), Petrograd and Leningrad. Long after her death it reverted to its original name.

This poem appears to follow the structure and flow of the kondak, the traditional Orthodox liturgical hymn of which Akhmatova was enamored. In this there is a kind of introduction, in which the drama unfolds, leading to a concluding and soothing consolation.

Life itself presents these three epochs, yet we may have difficulty recognizing ourselves as we pass from one to another. There is misery but, in the end, there remains the twist of hope.

OSIP MANDELSTAM (1891-1938) spent two years studying at universities in Paris and Heidelberg. He was close to both Gumilev and Akhmatova. He returned to Russia in 1911 but, seeing as there was a strict quota for Jews to be admitted to university, he was converted by a Methodist minister in Vyborg, a town in the USSR close to the border with Finland.

He was a self-declared Acmeist and considered the movement a vehicle for the moral rebirth of Russia. His colleagues called him "the marble fly" for his ability to cover a wide territory in his poetic wanderings and still appear to be both noble and timeless.

His most momentous lifetime encounter was with Nadezhda Khazina in 1919. They married some two years later. At a time when it was ultimately dangerous to write down some poems, Nadezhda committed them to memory and, by doing so, eventually preserved his legacy. She was also to write two volumes of memoirs that became popular outside her country. They were titled in English *Hope Against Hope* and *Hope Abandoned*. The name Nadezhda means "hope."

Mandelstam's poems are beautifully constructed, like exquisite jewelry with jewels of many facets. They are fiendishly difficult to translate in all their suggestiveness and subtlety. Words seem to be organic entities that sprout meanings and throw off spores, taking on a new life of their own. In his short poem about the town where he and Nadezhda were sent into exile, Voronezh, there are plays on words with both the name of the town, the Russian word for "raven" and the symbol of the black cars that abduct people to prison, camps and, often, their death.

Mandelstam was arrested primarily because his poem "We Live Apart from Our Land," translated below, came into the hands of officials thanks to a "friend" who, having heard it, wrote it down and reported him. This poem is often referred to as the "Stalin Epigram." Under torture and interrogation, Mandelstam did not deny that he was its author and even went so far as to pen it for his interrogators.

He was arrested in May 1938 and, four months later, sent east to the gulag. He died of exposure and, presumably, starvation before he got there.

I love two lines he wrote that are full of hope …

> *We will come together again in St. Petersburg*
> *As if we had buried the sun there*

TAKE FROM MY PALMS FOR YOUR HAPPINESS
OSIP MANDELSTAM

Take from my palms for your happiness
A sliver of sun and some drops of honey
As Persephone's bees demanded.

You cannot untie an unfastened boat.
You cannot hear a shadow shod in fur.
You cannot conquer fear in the thickets of life.

What's left for us ... only kisses
Furry, like little bees
Who die, having flown from their hive.

They rustle about in night's transparent underbrush
The dense Peloponnese forests their country
Feeding on honeysuckle, mint and time.

Now take my wild gift for your happiness!
This parched unattractive necklace
Made of dead bees who changed honey into a sun.

This poem was, alas, not dedicated to Nadezhda but rather to another woman he loved, the actor Olga Hildebrandt, whose stage surname was Arbenina. They met in 1920 and Mandelstam was smitten, though at the time she was seeing Gumilev.

This poem details the promise of a joyous and erotic love, but the undertone is tragic. Mandelstam was well aware of the old myth that bees die when they turn honey into a sun.

WE LIVE APART FROM OUR LAND
OSIP MANDELSTAM

We live apart from our land
Our words dying at ten paces
And anything put edgewise
Concerns the Kremlin backwoodsman.
His coarse fingers are thick, like worms
His statements trusty, like weights on a scale.
Cockroaches smile on his upper lip
And the rims of his shoes blind.

He is surrounded by a flock of pencil-neck hacks.
He plays on the servility of half-men
Who whistle, who meow, who sob.
But he alone roars and sticks it in
Forging his edicts like so many horseshoes
One in the groin, one on the brow, one in the eye.
Execution is his relish, this southerner
With an open heart.

This is the so-called Stalin Epigram. There is no mistaking who it is about. It was written in November 1933.

IMPRESSIONISM
OSIP MANDELSTAM

The artist has given us a portrait
Of lilacs in a trance.
He's placed sonorous steps of color
On a canvas, like scabs.

He understood the richness of oils.
His summer has coagulated
Warmed in a lilac brain
Spreading out to stifle the air.

Its shadow is a deeper mauve
A whistle, a whip, a match gone out.
You'll say, "It's the cooks in the kitchen
Dressing their oily pigeons."

You'll sense the presence of a swing
A thin sketch of veils.
But in this sunny breakdown
It's the bumblebee that reigns.

"Impressionism" was written in 1932, after Mandelstam had seen Monet's "Lilacs in the Sun" at the Pushkin Museum of Fine Arts in Moscow. In this poem he has given sound to color. Could there be a more beautiful description of an impressionist's work than one in which a presence of objects is sensed in a breakdown of light?

THERE WERE EYES
OSIP MANDELSTAM

There were eyes sharper than a whetted scythe
A puppy in the pupil and a droplet of dew ...

And having come of age, they only just learned
To distinguish one in a solitary mass of stars.

Some twenty years ago I was asked to translate a poem to post on the walls of the London tube under a program called "Poems on the Underground." I sent this one thinking that people on a train or a platform wouldn't have time to read a longer poem. To me this terse and intriguingly enigmatic poem describes a manner of poetic seeing, a metaphor illustrating the phrase "an eye for detail."

ALEXANDER BLOK (1880-1921) was every woman's and every man's poetic idol, so much so that the Silver Age of Russian poetry is popularly thought to have begun with the publication of his "Verses about a Lovely Lady" in 1904 and ending in his death. (The Golden Age took place in the first half of the nineteenth century and is generally associated with the work of Pushkin.) Blok was so adored and pursued by women that he became known as "the Don Juan of the North"; and postcards of him, with his curly blond hair and ethereal gray eyes sold by the tens of thousands. Not many poets have enjoyed that kind of a following!

Though the two poems I have chosen here are lyrical and full of nostalgia for faith and for his eternal city, St. Petersburg, Blok had a vehemently epic side as well, as seen in two of his poems, "The Twelve" and "Scythians." "The Twelve" mixes Bolshevik images with Christian ones. There have been competing narrative analyses of this long poem, and it is a toss up whether Christ is leading the Communists or vice versa. But as a dynamic poem with a mixture of the old and new faiths, it certainly symbolizes the patent bifurcation of history in Russia at the time. There is no doubt, however, that by the year of his death, 1921, Blok had determined that Bolshevism was the enemy of inner peace and creative freedom. He said as much in a speech at an immensely important event held in honor of Pushkin's memory in February of that year.

Blok had identified with an Asian (and Slavophile) Russia in "Scythians" in his country's eternally perceived confrontation with the West. It is these two faces of the nation, one vying with the other for space and attention before history's mirror, that have characterized Russia's spiritual dilemma from the time of Peter the Great to that of his self-appointed presumptive little heir, Vladimir Putin.

In any case, Blok's influence on his contemporaries and subsequent poets is immeasurable. When he died of endocarditis (a condition exacerbated by physical weakness: Blok was mentally at the end of his tether and barely eating) on 7 August 1921 his city went into mourning. Some 1,500 people followed the coffin, held on the shoulders of pall bearers that included Zamyatin and Bely. Russian composer Arthur Lourié remarked, "The Russian Revolution came to an end with Blok's death."

When Gumilev was executed a couple of weeks later, Akhmatova wrote that that August was "like a yellow flame, like smoke." Everyone recognized it as the end of an era.

A GIRL WAS SINGING IN A CHURCH CHOIR
ALEXANDER BLOK

A girl was singing in a church choir
About all weary people in a foreign land
About all the ships that had gone to sea
About all those who'd lost sight of rapture.

Her voice flew up to the top of the dome
As a ray of light shone on her pretty white shoulder
And everyone there stood listening in the dark
And watched as her white dress sang in that light.

And they all believed that joy was upon them
And that all the ships had found a calm bay
That all weary people so far, far away
Had found for themselves a radiant life.

Her voice was sweet, and the light so fine
That only on high, by the Holy Gates
Was a child weeping, aware of the secret
That no one at all would be coming back home.

Blok wrote "A Girl Was Singing in a Church Choir" in August 1905 in reference to
the revolution that began in January of that year and the loss of life to the Japanese in
the Tsushima Strait in May. In the poem he is foreshadowing the terrible tragedies

that accompany such traumatic historical events. He doesn't talk about political incidents or naval battles, but rather takes refuge in the symbolism that he finds in the church and the contrast of light and dark. It ends on a religious note with the child, privy to the awful secret, weeping.

I have a special fondness for this poem. I vividly remember linguist and literary historian Roman Jakobson, whose class at Harvard Graduate School I audited during the academic year 1964-65, reading this poem in Russian to us in his deep and sonorous voice, stepping back and forth as he read, as if dancing. I have loved this poem ever since.

NIGHT, THE STREET, THE LAMP, THE CHEMIST'S SHOP
ALEXANDER BLOK

Night, the street, the lamp, the chemist's shop
All in a dim and meaningless light.
Live for another quarter century
Nothing will change. There's no way out.

You'll die … you'll begin again once more.
Everything repeats itself, as before:
The night, the iced rippling on the canal
The chemist's shop, the street, and the same old lamp.

In "Night, the Street, the Lamp, the Chemist's Shop" Blok rejects the "new" world as it all but disappears into the fog of the old. This poem made an enormous impression on his fellow Symbolists. This was the beautiful old world that they saw themselves vanishing into. It dates from 1912 but reflects the depressive mood he fell into three years earlier when he lost both his father, with whom he had a very fond relationship, and his newborn son. At this point, at least, he is stuck in the old world with "no way out," and that's the way life is and always will be.

That his embrace of the revolution a few years later was half hearted can come as no surprise.

SERGEI ESENIN (1895-1925) was, by his own admission, "the last poet of the village." I have written extensive commentary on his life and times, together with translations of a large collection of his poetry, in my book *Wholly Esenin*, and would ask readers interested in delving into this most fascinating man to look to that book. I have included only a single poem of his here.

Like Blok, Esenin (pronounced Ye-SAY-nin) was utterly ambiguous about the revolution, now embracing, now rejecting it. He waxed supremely lyrical over his hometown in the Ryazan countryside while his true feelings about it waned conspicuously; he wrote exquisite love poetry, some of it scathing; he paraded about the big city decked out like a country bumpkin, yet donned fancy bourgeois dress when he toured Europe with his wife (one of what was altogether four of them), the American dancer Isadora Duncan.

In the end he had only contempt for the Russia that was marching mindlessly in step with wholesale industrialization. In "Sorokoust— Requiem for the Dead" he shows up the contrast in a brutal light …

> *Did you see how the train runs*
> *On its cast-iron hoofs*
> *Over the steppe … how it takes cover*
> *In the fogs of the lake*
> *How it snorts through iron nostrils?*
>
> *And just behind it gallops the colt*
> *Over the vast grassland*
> *In the reckless rush of a feast day*
> *With its red mane*
> *And its skinny legs angling toward its head.*
>
> *Darling, darling, laughable jackass*
> *What's the rush … and where to?*
> *Doesn't he know by now that the cavalry of steel*

Has already defeated living horses
And that his running through those darkening fields
Will not bring back the times when a nomad
Traded in a pair of gorgeous women of the steppe
For a horse?
The gnashing destiny of the marketplace
Has dyed this lifted stretch of land
And a locomotive is now worth
Thousands of pounds of horsemeat and hide.

Go to hell, you vulgar guest!
Our song will not adapt to you.

He refused and was unable to "adapt," and perhaps for that reason Esenin has remained all things to all Russians. That is why they love him, their own private Esenin, so much. His death by suicide (though some still blame the secret police) has been romanticized beyond all recognition. Some poetic purists may still be reluctant to take his verse seriously, but he remains arguably Russia's most popular twentieth-century poet.

He put succinctly what he thought it meant to be a poet …

To be a poet, if you do not wish
To violate life's truths
You need to scar your tender skin and caress
People's hearts in the emotions of your blood.

I'll refrain from commenting on "Poem about a Dog." The story it tells is clear.

POEM ABOUT A DOG

SERGEI ESENIN

In the morning, in the barn for rye
Where rush mats stand in golden rows
She gave birth to a litter of seven
Seven newborn chestnut-color pups.

She fondled them until the evening came
Licking them all over
As the snow melted into trickles
Under the warmth of her belly.

But in the evening, when the hens
Sit restfully on their perches
The grim master appeared
And dropped all seven puppies into a sack.

The mother raced over the snowdrifts
Not letting the master get ahead.
And for ages the smooth surface of water
Unfrozen, would not cease its trembling.

And when, in the end, she dragged herself back
Licking the moisture off her flanks

She took the moon, shining over the shack
For one of her puppies.

She gazed up into the dark blue sky
Whining for all she was worth.
But the thin moon slipped behind a hill
Disappearing beyond the fields.

And just as when they mock her
By tossing a stone at her instead of food
Her eyes rolled silently
Like golden stars into the snow.

MARINA TSVETAEVA (1892-1941) is now considered on par with Akhmatova for her verse expressing the inner passions and outer struggles of women. If Akhmatova is the poet of St. Petersburg, Tsvetaeva is the voice of Moscow. Both Bryusov (see page 60) and Gumilev praised her early poems, the former noting that they made readers feel ill at ease, as if they were observing an intimate scene that should normally be inaccessible to them. In that sense, Tsvetaeva's poetry is starkly revelatory, opening our eyes to things we may sense are there but hadn't been able to put our finger on and grasp.

Tsvetaeva married Sergei Efron when she was twenty and he, nineteen. She identified with the anti-Bolshevik cause, largely, it seems, because her husband fought in the White Army. This was to cause her much trouble in later years. They spent their fifteen years outside Russia, primarily in Prague, Berlin and, the longest span, Paris, almost entirely in penury. She had gone into exile in 1922 after losing her daughter to hunger during the Civil War that followed the revolution. She had another daughter who left Russia with her, and a son was born in 1925 (he was killed in the war in 1944).

While in the Czech capital she started up a three-way correspondence with Boris Pasternak and the Bohemian Austrian poet Rainer Maria Rilke. After the latter's death in December 1926 she continued exchanging letters with Pasternak, but the two were not to meet until her return to the USSR.

She frequented the famous—and still popular to this day—Café Slavia, located opposite the National Theater and not far from the offices of the émigré magazine "Russia's Will," one of whose editors— and later editor-in-chief—was the remarkable critic, scholar and translator Mark Slonim, who published Tsvetaeva and believed in her.

It was while in what was then Czechoslovakia that she had a passionate affair with an officer, Konstanty Rodziewicz (whose name is given incorrectly in many sources). It was for him that she wrote her beautiful "Poem of the Mountain," in which she tells us …

Passion is no delusion, no fiction
And it doesn't lie ... but it is fleeting!
If only we had come into this world
As simple commoners of love!

She uses the word *prostolyudin* in the last line, which can indicate peasant as well as commoner, in effect, someone who is not from the nobility or gentry. I love her book *My Pushkin*, in which she states that had she been alive a century earlier she would have longed to be Pushkin's wet nurse rather than his lover.

Tsvetaeva's husband Sergei Efron was, in the meantime, turning himself into a Soviet spy. He returned to his homeland in October 1937 but was arrested in 1939, held in jail, sentenced in August 1941—though he swore that "I was not a spy; I was an honest agent of Soviet intelligence"—and executed two months later.

Tsvetaeva returned home in 1939. Destitute and ignored, she evacuated from Moscow in 1941, ending up in the small town of Yelabuga in the Republic of Tatarstan, two hundred kilometers east of Kazan. Shunned by the literary community, both official and nonofficial, and unable to find any type of work save the most menial, she hanged herself on a hook over the doorstep of her hut in Yelabuga. The daughter who had returned with her father was arrested and not released until 1955, spending in all sixteen years as a prisoner of her own people.

Tsvetaeva was born into privilege: Her father founded the museum that later became the renowned Pushkin Museum, and her mother was a concert pianist. But her life in Russia and abroad was perhaps the most tragic of any contemporary literary figure. And yet her poetry is infused with immense positive passion and a vitriolic power.

AN ATTEMPT AT JEALOUSY
MARINA TSVETAEVA

How are you getting on with your new woman?
Life's simpler, is it? The oar strikes!
And soon memories recede
With the coastline.

Memories of me are
An island drifting away
(into the sky … not over waves!)
Kindred spirits, you two
Sisters, not lovers!

How are you getting on with that plain woman
The one without a spot of the divine?
You've pulled the throne from under me
Deposed your queen.

How are you getting on, do you fuss over her?
Do you shiver when you open your eyes in the morning?
How are you paying the duty, poor man
On such eternal vulgarity?

"I've had my fill of intermittent hysterics.
I'll rent myself a house."

How are you getting along with that other woman
You, whom I chose to be mine?

And how's the food, more to your taste?
Don't blame me if it turns your stomach.
How is it living with a faded copy of a woman
You who reached the summit of Sinai?

How are you getting on with your stranger
Your local girl? Do you love your little Eve?
Aren't you ashamed to wear the scar
Of Zeus's strap on your forehead?

How are you getting on? Are you feeling well?
Do you sing, and if so, how do you sound?
How, poor man, do you deal with the ulcer
Of an eternal curse on your conscience?

How are you getting on with your piece of meat
From the market? Will her value hold?
After Carrara marble
How are you living with plaster

Dust? (God was carved from a stone block
But it shattered just like that!)
How are you getting on with your run-of-the-mill woman
After you've known Lilith?

You've had enough, have you, of your market novelty?

Do her tricks leave you cold?

How are you getting on with the mundane

Woman who lacks six

Senses?

So, out with it, are you happy?

No? How then are you living, darling

In your shallow hole? Are you as miserable

As I am with my new man?

"An Attempt at Jealousy" is one of Tsvetaeva's most famous poems. She had numerous affairs with men and women but always managed to find her way back to her husband. It was written in 1924, some months after she broke up with her officer-lover Konstanty Rodziewicz. In it she vents her ire with sarcasm and style. By calling this an "attempt," she is demonstrating that she would not stoop to be truly jealous … though she is so convincing, she may be fooling herself more than him or us.

Lilith was Adam's first wife in the Bible and is depicted in many paintings—some of which Tsvetaeva would have been familiar with—as a sexy temptress.

READERS OF NEWSPAPERS
MARINA TSVETAEVA

The underground snake is crawling
Crawling with people on its back.
They all have their own newspaper
(Their own type of eczema)
Their ruminant nervous tic
Their newspaper bone decay.
Chewers of varnish resin
Readers of newspapers.

Who's reading? An old man? An athlete?
A soldier? Featureless, faceless
Ageless, a skeleton, after all
No face, just a sheet
Of newspaper! A sheet that all Paris
Puts on from its brow to its belly button.
Stop while you can, young girl.
You'll give birth to a reader of newspapers!

Swag… "She lives with her sister"
…ger … "He murdered his father!"
They swagger, puffed up
On airs and arrogance.

Those gentlemen can't tell the difference
Between dawn and dusk
Gluttons of emptiness
Readers of newspapers!

Read your newspapers: Libel!
Read your newspapers: Embezzlement!
A column here of malicious gossip
A paragraph there of rot.

What will you bring to light
On your own Judgement Day?
You grabbers of minutes
You readers of newspapers!

Scram! Get lost! Vanish!
Ancient maternal fear.
Oh Mother, Guttenberg's printing press
Is more frightening than Berthold the Black's alchemy!

You're more at home in a village cemetery
Than in a festering infirmary
You scratchers of pustules
You readers of newspapers!

Who is rotting our sons
In the prime of their years?

You who stir the blood
You who write for newspapers!

Yes, my friends, you're more robust
Than my lines, stronger
Than my thoughts, as I hold
My manuscript in my hands.

I stand before his face
A void like no other
That is, the total facelessness
Of the editor of news …
… paper Evil: the No-ah of slag and froth.

"Readers of Newspapers" was written in November 1935 but it strikes me as applying equally to our world today and could readily be retitled "Readers of Tabloids" or "Scanners of Social Media."

This poem illustrates Tsvetaeva's experimental use of language, mixing registers and disjointing her words and phrases with a pumping staccato rhythm. Even mothers don't escape her venom here: They will give birth to low life (i.e. readers of newspapers).

The reference to newspapers stirring the blood may well be prompted by the seizure of Abyssinia by Italian troops in 1935, an event that Tsvetaeva saw as a portent of world war (and she was right). The theme of war and violence is evident here as well: soldier, bones, skeleton, infirmary. Berthold the Black was a fourteenth-century alchemist who it was thought at the time, and for some subsequent centuries, had invented gunpowder, another reference here to war.

VALERY BRYUSOV (1873-1924), scholar, novelist, playwright, critic, translator, publisher, editor and a poet generally considered the father of Russian symbolism scandalized his country's literary establishment in the summer of 1895 with his five-word poem, "O close your pale legs" (*O zakroi svoi blednye nogi*). The scandal emerged due to the poem's eroticism, but it was also fed by a hot controversy as to whether these five words constituted a real poem or not. Whatever, with seven syllables in Russian short of a haiku, it is terse.

This set the tone for Bryusov's poetry, much of which is about love and other forms of intimacy. It is hard to think of the two great symbolists Blok and Bely (see page 68) without Bryusov's influence. He himself was deeply influenced by the French symbolists, particularly Verlaine, whose poems he was the first person to translate into Russian. Among many other translations that he did—of Goethe, Hugo, Poe, Wilde, to name a few—were those of Armenian poets, whose cause he championed. He published a large volume of old and modern Armenian poets titled *The Poetry of Armenia*. In 1916 he went to St. Petersburg to give a speech celebrating the book's publication, becoming an instant hero of the Armenian community in Russia.

Bryusov enjoyed great popularity in his later years, when he became, in 1910, literary editor of the popular magazine "Russian Thought" and, during World War I, its war correspondent. (He was shocked by the carnage that he saw and had a nervous breakdown.)

He was slow to embrace Bolshevism but joined the Communist Party in 1920, which estranged him from many in the literary community. The new government gave him a position overseeing culture. It wasn't long before he saw the wanton destruction that the Bolsheviks were wreaking on Russia's old culture and lost enthusiasm for the regime, falling into a deep depression and dying of pneumonia at age fifty. After all, his family had been very well to do, and he had enjoyed many privileges as a young man and had attended Moscow University. What sort of future could such an avant-garde and advantaged artist have in Soviet Russia?

His 1907 novel *The Republic of the Southern Cross* is one of the earliest examples of a dystopian narrative in literature. It is set in Zvezdny ("Star Town"), located at the South Pole. Despite the harsh conditions, the population of the town grows to two and a half million, among a total population in the republic of fifty million. The republic boasts electric lights, heating and an overhead railway (sixty percent of the population are metal workers). This republic is in every way a utopia with the trappings of a democracy. But it displays the realities of a totalitarian dictatorship. Everyone wears the same clothes and eats the same food; and, although there is universal suffrage, every candidate put up by the government is elected. This "republic" sounds eerily like more than one twenty-first-century nation.

But the citizenry is stricken by a terrible disease that causes them to rebel against all rules and regulations. This reaches epidemic proportions, until everyone there has caught the disease. The symptoms cause everyone to act in a contrary manner: Train conductors pay people to ride on their trains; newspaper proofreaders make deliberate and absurd mistakes; nurses slit patients' throats.

People start to flee en masse to Australia and Patagonia. Chaos ensues as citizens stampede all modes of transport. Violent incidents abound and suicide is rampant. All hell breaks loose and infrastructure collapses into madness and terror. In the end, amid the massive devastation, some signs of life and commerce emerge, and tourists begin visiting the republic to gawk at the spectacle of decimation.

That the author of *The Republic of the Southern Cross* turned to Bolshevism little more than a decade after writing this amazing novella is rather astounding. But Bryusov, erudite scholar and poet of erotic verse, classicist, historian and war correspondent, encompassed every contradiction of his time, the very embodiment of an era of transition from the old Russia into something new but terrifyingly destructive.

Today there is a Bryusov Lane in the center of Moscow about four hundred meters from the Bolshoi Theater.

THE BLESSING

VALERY BRYUSOV

I bless the radiant glow in your eyes.
It shone through my delirium.

I bless the smile on your lips.
It made me drunk, like wine.

I bless the venom in your kisses.
It poisoned all my thoughts, my dreams.

I bless the sickle of your embraces.
You reaped my past with it.

I bless the fire of your love.
I gladly fell into its flames.

I bless all the darkness in your soul.
It stretched its wings all over me.

I bless you for everything … everything
For the sorrow, the pain, the dread of drawn-out days

And for leading me to the gates of Paradise
And leaving me there to freeze.

"The Blessing," written in 1908, was headed by a quotation of a bon mot by the French symbolist poet Remy de Gourmont, that clearly inspired Bryusov: May your hands be blessed/For they are unclean.

DON'T CRY, DON'T THINK

VALERY BRYUSOV

Don't cry, don't think.
The past does not exist.
The light of dawn is bursting
With a welcoming blast.

You fell asleep and died
But came to life with morning.
Behold the distant sky
Without a thought in your head.

What's eternal is wished for.
What's harsh will die.
Don't stay in place, go forward
Unceasingly … unceasingly.

Bryusov wrote "Don't Cry, Don't Think" in 1896.

KONSTANTIN BALMONT (1867-1942) was a symbolist poet and translator who fled his native land after vehemently opposing the new regime. While living earlier in St. Petersburg with his wife and daughter he was admired by many in the literary world. In fact, he was arguably the most popular symbolist poet around the turn of the twentieth century. His reputation was no less formidable outside Russia. In 1897 he was invited to Oxford to give lectures on Russian poetry.

Balmont became somewhat notorious in March 1901 when he recited his poem "The Little Sultan," an outright attack on Tsar Nicholas II—"One little Sultan who is not very smart"—as a protest against the suppression of student protest. Then, during the 1905 revolution, packing a pistol and giving fiery speeches, he was compelled to flee Russia for Paris at the end of that year, remaining abroad for more than seven years and only returning in 1913, when, in February, the House of Romanov celebrated their three hundred years on the throne with a general amnesty.

Balmont continued to travel, however, making his way across Russia to Japan. He left Russia for good in May 1920; and, in ensuing years, exile only reinforced his anti-Soviet stance.

Tempestuous family life—with three wives, two of them common law—and at least two attempts at suicide led to an existence in France that by the 1930s was destitute and without recognition. Balmont suffered from serious depression, this man who had once been the most celebrated of Russian poets by his contemporaries. He never ceased longing for his native land.

Balmont was buried in a cemetery in Noisy-le-Grand, a commune in the eastern districts of Paris. Perhaps these words that he wrote in an essay in 1895 speak most clearly of his aspirations ...

No, I don't want to cry on and on. No, I want to be free. ... To rise up to the heights means to be higher than you yourself are. To rise to the heights is to be reborn. I know that one cannot always be on top. But I will return to the people; I will descend so that I can tell people what I saw high above. … Let me embrace for an instant with solitude; let me breathe with the wind of freedom!

I CAME INTO THIS WORLD TO SEE THE SUN
KONSTANTIN BALMONT

I came into this world to see the sun
And the dark-blue horizon below it.
I came into this world to see the sun
And the summits of mountains.

I came into this world to see the sea
And the lush colors of valleys.
I enwrap worlds in a single gaze.
I am a sovereign.

I have vanquished frigid oblivion
And created my own dream.
My every moment brings revelation
And I never cease to sing.

Suffering has awakened the dream in me
But I am loved for that.
Who can equal my lyrical power?
No one … not a soul.

I entered this world to see the sun.
But if the day dies out
I will sing of the sun, sing of the sun
In my vanishing breath.

Balmont wrote "I Came into this World to See the Sun" in 1903, when he was at the height of his popularity. He uses the word *vlastelin*, which I have translated with "a sovereign." The denotation of this word, which derives from the Russian word for "power," is "absolute ruler", but it can also imply figuratively that someone is a master of something. The Russian translation of "Lord" in Tolkien's *Lord of the Rings* uses *vlastelin*. Balmont was his own master and a poet who, despite the abyss that was his final years, refused to give in to darkness.

ANDREI BELY (1880-1934) was, in his day, one of the most celebrated poets and novelists. Nabokov famously valued his novel about a lone terrorist, *St. Petersburg*, as one of the greatest novels of the twentieth century. Bely, a dyed-in-the-wool Muscovite, presents a pretty unpleasant portrait of Russia's old capital, and some natives of the city responded by dismissing this portrait as insulting. Akhmatova praised the novel but did not consider it a realistic depiction of her beloved city. (Perhaps writers from St. Petersburg knew that Bely saw their city as the symbol of a decadent West that was bound to implode and disappear. In *St. Petersburg* the city does just that, fall into a hole. Bely predicted in print that the discoveries of Madame Curie would someday lead to the manufacture of a nuclear bomb. Perhaps, then, he foresaw Akhmatova's beloved city falling into a black hole.)

Bely (whose name is often transliterated with Biely and is pronounced Bee-EH-lee) was an experimenter in language and style and is often compared to James Joyce, though the latter's prose is much more linguistically deconstructed than Bely's. *St. Petersburg* plots a chase by a terrorist to locate a government official. It mixes arch-realism with surrealistic twists, mystical thoughts with parodies of mystical thoughts and, in all, takes off where Gogol left off. It also stands as a precursor of later Soviet magic realism, especially as seen in Bulgakov's *The Master and Margarita*, a fine novel but, to my mind, just a patch on the fabric woven by Bely.

His mystic and prophetic novel that was written four years before *St. Petersburg, The Silver Dove*, is one of the books that eloquently counters the naturalism, both in theme and style, of the nineteenth-century Russian novel. Perhaps the Russian novelist that he most closely resembled was Boris Pilnyak, equally an experimenter who took up themes relating to the contrast between city and country life.

He was not entirely ill disposed toward the revolution but nevertheless went abroad to Germany in 1921, staying two years. He embraced anthroposophy and worshipped its founder, Rudolf Steiner, whom he met a few times before and after the revolution.

Bely's love life was complicated by two triangular relationships, one with Bryusov and Nina Petrovskaya; the other with Alexander Blok and his wife Lyubov Mendeleeva. (Mendeleeva went back to her husband, who wrote a play about the whole affair. Bryusov's book about his triangular affair with Petrovskaya at the vertex was a novel written in 1907, *The Fiery Angel*, which was later turned into an opera by Prokofiev. The opera was performed in Paris in 1954, a year after its composer's death, and again in Venice in 1955.)

But Bely went on to marry Turgenev's grand-niece Anna (whom he called "Asya"), who also became a Steiner devotee. Bely went abroad again, leaving Asya in Russia. She decided to devote her life to Steiner's philosophy, becoming what she called an "anthroposophical nun." Bely, none too chuffed by this turn of events, fell into a depressive state and wrote love poems to her. Bely and Asya divorced, and Bely married Klavdiya Vasilyeva after she was able to divorce her husband in 1929. Klavdiya, who was also a follower of Steiner, stayed with Bely until the end. She herself passed away in 1970, after having written a memoir about him.

When Bely died in 1934, many poets paid tribute to him in verse and prose, including Mandelstam and Pasternak.

THE WIZARD

ANDREI BELY

I am inside the whistling hiss of time's currents
My black raincoat, rebellious, shreds
I summon the people. I seek out the prophets
Who can sing of the celestial secret

I forge ahead with a swift pace
And find you, patient wizard, perched on a cliff
Watching with your crown of stars
And a prophetic smile

A discordant rumble roars and rebels
In an eternal dream at the foot of centuries
And your voice reaches to the freezing heights
Like an eagle's high-pitched screech

The frozen wizard has folded arms
This prophet of a timeless spring
In his crown of fire he's risen above the realm
Of both the weary and of time itself

"The Wizard" was dedicated to Valery Bryusov. It was written after 1904, when Bely had left Russia after his lover, Lyubov, had gone back to her husband. He spent the better part of four years in Western Europe, mostly in Munich and Paris. In this poem he seems to be looking for the answer of how to take control of time by seeking out a supernatural force and rising above "the realm."

VLADISLAV KHODASEVICH (1886-1939) was a poet and critic. Nabokov called him "the great Russian poet of our time" (Khodasevich was one of the few major Russian literary figures in emigration who understood Nabokov's importance to Russian and world literature). Writers as different as Gumilev and Gorky also publicly recognized his genius.

Khodasevich was married to the Armenian Russian author Nina Berberova. I met her in 1967, visited her country home in Connecticut and heard at that time much about him and others in their circle. They had met at the end of 1921 (Khodasevich had separated from his first wife), and in the summer of 1922 they left Russia for Berlin.

Khodasevich had flirted with communism in the early months of the revolution but soon disparaged it for its curtailing of literary freedom. Subsequently he and Nina made the move from Berlin to Paris, as many Russian intellectuals outside Russia were doing. They spent much time in the company of Bely, Gorky, Jakobson and Nabokov. The renaissance in culture in Russia that they had hoped for was not to materialize. They separated in April 1932. Nina Berberova emigrated to the United States in 1950 and taught at both Yale and Princeton. She died in 1993, at the age of ninety-two.

In the 1920s and 1930s Khodasevich worked on a memoir that he eventually published under the title *Necropolis*, so named because he believed that Soviet Russia had buried its great poets of the Silver Age, some figuratively, mostly literally. He also wrote in the book about Andrei Bely's love triangles. He had been taught by Bryusov and knew his wife Nina Petrovskaya, the woman involved in the love triangle with Bely. Petrovskaya stayed with Khodasevich and Berberova in Paris, but by then she was on the skids, reliant on drugs and living in penury. She took her own life at a Salvation Army refuge in Paris in February 1928. *Necropolis* tells it all—emigration, revolution and its rejection, poetry, art, survival and the suppression or death of poets like Gumilev and Esenin.

In a telling poem written at the end of 1917, when two realities coexisted in his country, Khodasevich wrote ...

> *Look for me in the sheer light of spring*
> *I am it all: like a flap of imperceptible wings*
> *I am sound, I am breath*
> *I am a spot of reflected light on a parquet floor*
> *I am lighter than that spot*
> *It exists, there ... while I am in the past*

Khodasevich's second wife, Olga Borisovna Margolina-Khodasevich, published her own memoir in French in 1941. But being Jewish, she was soon sent, via the Drancy internment camp, to Auschwitz, where she was killed in September 1942. She was the niece of Mark Aldanov, the émigré novelist who was nominated for the Nobel Prize for Literature thirteen times, six of the nominations having come from Nobel laureate Ivan Bunin.

Khodasevich wrote that he carried his Russia around in his traveling case, a convenient container for a peripatetic exile. He beautifully summarized the role—or yoke—of the poet writing in any language when he wrote: "The gift of secret hearing is heavy."

I LOVE PEOPLE, I LOVE NATURE

VLADISLAV KHODASEVICH

I love people, I love nature.
But I hate to just go for a walk
And am convinced that my people
Cannot fathom my creations

I don't require much, and weigh
What ungenerous fate has dealt me:
The elm that inclines towards the barn
The hillock blanketed by a forest

I expect neither crude fame
Nor persecution from my contemporaries
And I rely on no one to prune the lilac bushes
Surrounding my terrace and growing in my garden

ALEXANDER PUSHKIN (1799-1837) is Russia's eternal poet laureate. His great-great-grandfather was Abram Petrovich Hannibal, a black African born, it is thought, in Cameroon around the end of the seventeenth century. Hannibal was taken to Moscow. His patronymic came from his godfather, Peter the Great. He rose to be general-in-chief of the Russian Army. Pushkin was proud of his African heritage.

Outside Russia, Pushkin is probably most well known for his novel in verse, *Eugene Onegin*, which was turned into an opera by Tchaikovsky. In Russia his poems still enjoy huge popularity and are considered the template of the classic.

He was something of a wild fellow, and his racy quips and smutty epithets put a smirk on the lips of many a Russian school-age child.

I've chosen two poems by him to illustrate the consummate lyricism and the satirical sting in his work.

Pushkin was shot in the abdomen in a duel and died two days later from the wound.

I RECALL A MIRACULOUS MOMENT

ALEXANDER PUSHKIN

I recall a miraculous moment
When you appeared before me
Like a passing, fleeting vision
The epitome of purest grace

Your tender voice remained in me
As I suffered from hopeless grief
As raucous trifles troubled me
I dreamt of your exquisite features

Years passed, restless gusts
Scattered old dreams to the wind
And I could not recall your tender voice
Or your every heavenly feature

My days dragged on in a lull
In empty gloom, imprisonment
With neither faith nor inspiration
Nor tears, nor life, nor love

But then my soul came back to life
And you appeared before me
Like a passing fleeting vision
The epitome of purest grace

And now my heart beats rapturously
My soul has quickened again
In faith, in inspiration
In tears, in life, in love

YOU, YOU LOW-LIFE LIARS
ALEXANDER PUSHKIN

You, flaming-hot Muse of Satire
Save your rattling lyre
And hand over Juvenal's Whip instead!
My poetic barbs are not aimed
At frigid imitators
Or starving translators
Or sheep-like rhymesters
Peace to you, pathetic poets
Peace to you, magazine minions
Peace to you, meek dolts
But you, you low-life liars
Step forward! I'll shame you all
I'll torment your bastard hearts!

But if I overlook one of you, Gentlemen
Please make yourself known to me
So many shameless pale faces
So many blockhead brows
Are simply asking
For my indelible brand

Juvenal is the Roman satirist whose *Sixteen Satires* remains the classic of this literary genre. "Juvenal's Whip" is an epithet indicating the lashes of well-placed satire.

FYODOR TYUTCHEV (1803-1873) was a poet and diplomat who in his lifetime achieved great fame and recognition for his gifts, rising to high rank in the diplomatic service.

His poems are clear in style, accessible and not overly wordy; and he is, at core, a Romantic. Pushkin had a hand in establishing his career when he included some of his poems in the journal he was editing, *Sovremennik* (The Contemporary).

Many of Tyutchev's poems depict the seas, a fact that reflects his many days spent on them ...

> *As the ocean embraces the globe*
> *Life on earth is embraced by dreams*
> *Day turns to night, and water strikes*
> *Its shore with resounding waves*

FINAL LOVE

FYODOR TYUTCHEV

Oh how much more tender and irrational
Is the love we feel on the cliff of our years …
Shine bright, shine bright, farewell light
Of final twilight love!
A shadow has overtaken half the sky
Only there in the west is a flitting glow …
Slow down, slow down, close of day
Last longer, magic loveliness!
Though the blood in our veins runs thinner with time
The tenderness in our heart remains full …
And you, final—ultimate—love
You are my sole bliss and my sole despair

It's hard to imagine a more poignant outlook on old age. The sky is already half in shadow and the only light comes from the setting sun … and even that is only flitting. The sentiment is different from that in Dylan Thomas's urging to his father—to not go gentle "into that good night"—but his plea to the day's end to "slow down" and "last longer" in its "magic loveliness" strikes a similar chord.

CICERO

FYODOR TYUTCHEV

for Giorgio Amitrano

The Roman orator spoke
Amidst alarming civil storms:
"I arose late and was overtaken on the road
By the night of Rome"
You were! But you saw from the Capitoline heights
The city's bloody star go down
In all its greatness
As you bade farewell to its glory
Fortunate are those who have visited this world
In its fateful and ruinous moments
They have been invited by the gods
To take a seat at the feasting table
To be eye witness to the lofty spectacle
And alive, as one in Paradise
You drank from their immortal cup

I have no doubt but that Tyutchev was thinking not only of Cicero's Rome but also of his precious homeland (he was an ardent Slavophile) when he wrote, somewhat counterintuitively, about the good fortune of those who experience fateful—and ruinous—times. The Russian word used here is *rokovye* (in its plural form), which derives from the word for "fate" and has the connotation of "fatal." "Ruinous," in its association with ancient Rome, seemed an apt additional modifier.

IVAN TURGENEV (1818-1883) was, in his own day, Russia's most popular and most thoroughly Westernized author. His prose style is lucid and naturalistic, and the themes that he took up inspired narratives of writers in Russia and around the world in the last decades of the nineteenth and the early twentieth centuries. It is impossible to think of the plays of Anton Chekhov without the inspiration of Turgenev's play about a superficially satiated and bored gentry, "A Month in the Country."

Turgenev's biting satirical side is evident in the following prose-poem that he wrote in July 1878, "The Journalist." It was the previous year that he began creating in this genre as a kind of "lyrical diary."

THE JOURNALIST

IVAN TURGENEV

Two friends were seated at a table having tea when suddenly a loud noise accosted them from the street. Then they heard plaintive groaning, violent swearing, outbursts of malicious laughter.

"Someone's getting beaten up," remarked one of the friends, glancing out the window.

"A criminal? A murderer?" asked the other. "Listen, we can't permit such harsh illegal treatment, whoever the guy is."

"But it's not a murderer who's getting beaten up."

"Not a murderer? So, it's a thief? Anyway, that's not the point. We should go out and separate him from the mob."

"But he's not a thief, I tell you!"

"He's not a thief? Maybe he's a cashier, a supervisor on the railways, a contractor for the military, a Russian patron of the arts, a lawyer, a well-meaning editor, a welfare donor? It doesn't matter, we should go and help him!"

"No … it's a journalist they're doing over."

"A journalist? Well, in that case, look. What d'ya say we finish drinking our tea first."

NIKOLAI NEKRASOV (1821-1878) was not only extremely popular among the common people in his lifetime but also had achieved establishment recognition in the very top rank of Russian poets. He served as editor of influential journals, among them *Sovremennik* as a successor to Pushkin. He was Russia's great compassionate liberal. His poem describing a peasant woman being mercilessly whipped was an open challenge to the cruelty of Nicholas I's regime. In the poem he calls to the Muse to look upon this woman as her sister.

Toward the end of his life he published a long poem titled "Who's Happy in Russia?" It tells the story of the (unsuccessful) quest to find one single contented person in the whole country. All the seekers find is misery and injustice. This poem had a significant impact on future generations of progressive Russian intellectuals. D.S. Mirsky, the great historian of Russian literature, said of Nekrasov that "[his people] were not only an object of compassion and worship. He could sympathize with their humor and their laughter as well as their sufferings. Of all Russian poets of the nineteenth century he was the only one who was genuinely and creatively akin to the spirit of popular songs. He did not imitate them. He simply had in him the soul of a popular singer."

Dostoevsky delivered the eulogy at Nekrasov's funeral, saying that he came just after Pushkin and Lermontov in greatness. But young people, who looked to Nekrasov for inspiration in their struggle against censorship and the oppressive state, hollered, "No, he comes before Pushkin ... BEFORE!"

LULLABY
NIKOLAI NEKRASOV

Sleep, little brat, while you're still harmless
Bayushki-bayu.
The bronze moon is peering dimly
Into your sweet little cradle.
Now I will tell you not a tale
But sing the simple truth.
So close your eyes and doze away …
Bayushki-bayu.

A cry has resounded throughout the province
Gratifying all.
Your father's found himself in court
Smothered in blatant evidence.
But your father's only too aware
Of his role as a notable swindler.
So sleep, my little brat, while you're still honest.
Bayushki-bayu.

You'll grow up and soon you'll understand
The baptized world around you.
You'll buy a dark-green set of tails
And take a pen in hand.
You'll say: "I'm well intentioned
I stand for all that's good!"
So sleep, your future path is certain.
Bayushki-bayu.

You'll look the part, a bureaucrat
But deep down be a crook.
And I'll be there beside you
To wave my hand on high.
You'll fit in beautifully, you will
And work like the devil himself.
So sleep, my little devil, while you're innocent
Bayushki-bayu.

You'll be as gentle, meek as a lamb
With a head-butting little forehead.
And like a snake you'll slither
Into a soft and cushy job.
You'll look out for yourself, you will
And your own very special interests.
So sleep now while you cannot steal!
Bayushki-bayu.

You'll buy a multi-story house
And grab a high position.
And soon you'll be a VIP
A Russian aristocrat.
You'll live in peace and harmony
And someday you will die.
So sleep, my little functionary.
Bayushki … Bye-bye….

This is a parody of the 1838 poem "Cossack's Lullaby" by Mikhail Lermontov, which begins …

> *Sleep, my dearest little one*
> *Bayushki-bayu.*
> *The bright moon is peering silently*
> *Into your sweet little cradle*

On 8 January 1846 the chief censor A.V. Nikitenko put the question of Nekrasov's parody before the government censorship committee and the following resolution was adopted: "The committee, not finding anything contrary to the rules of censorship in this satirical poem, has decided to permit its publication." This lenient outcome certainly wouldn't have occurred a century later in 1946; and it very well might not in today's Russia either.

I DON'T FEEL SORRY FOR A FRIEND OR A WIFE
NIKOLAI NEKRASOV

I don't feel sorry for a friend or a wife
Or even for the hero himself
When noting down the horrors of war
And every new victim of bloodshed.
Alas, the wife will find her consolation.
The best friend will forget his mate.
But somewhere lives a single soul
Who'll remember till her dying day.

In all the hypocrisies of our affairs
And every form of prosaic vulgarity
I've detected the only tears in this world
Sublime and truly heartfelt.
Those are the tears of the pitiful mothers
Who cannot forget their sons
Slain on bloody fields of grain
Just as the weeping willow cannot stop
Her branches from hanging down.

This poem was written in 1865 referring back to the horrors of the Crimean War a decade earlier.

IVAN KRYLOV (1769-1844) was and still is Russia's most beloved fabulist, a kind of Aesop and H.C. Andersen rolled into one. He published his first book of fables in 1809, and by 1825 he was famous outside Russia as well. That was the year a collection of his fables was published in Paris in French and Italian. One of his translators was Claude Joseph Rouget de Lisle, who wrote the lyrics and music for what was to become La Marseillaise.

Krylov's first attempts at writing came in the form of playwrighting when he was sixteen. This sharpened his ear for dialogue. The speech in his fables is totally natural, a feat that not many poets and writers of prose achieve.

Krylov wrote, all in all, nearly two hundred fables, "The Quartet" being his most famous.

THE QUARTET
IVAN KRYLOV

A wily monkey
A donkey
A goat
And a ham-fisted bear
Decided to form a quartet.
They acquired a score, a bass
A viola and a couple of fiddles.
They sat down in a meadow under a linden tree
To charm the world with their art.
They plucked and sawed away but got nowhere fast.
"Stop, fellows, stop! Hold your horses!" cried the monkey.
"How can we make music if we're not sitting in proper places?
"You, bear, take your bass and sit opposite the viola.
I, as first violin, will sit opposite the second violin.
Then we will make such music together
That the woods and hills will dance to our tune!"
They took their seats and started their quartet.
But, even so, what came out was plain old noise.
"Stop it, I've worked out the secret!" screamed the donkey.
"If we sit in a line, everything will be fine."
They took his advice and sat in a row.
But once again, all they made was just more noise.
Now they quibbled and squabbled even more than before
About where and how to sit.

So, when a nightingale happened by, hearing the noise
They turned to her to resolve their doubts.
"Please," they said, "spare us a moment
To bring order to our quartet.
We've got the notes and instruments
But please do tell us how to sit!"
"To be a musician, you must have aptitude
And an ear more attuned than yours,"
Answered the nightingale.
"You, my friends, will never make music together
No matter what seat you sit yourselves in."

"The Quartet" is quoted in many everyday situations when people are squabbling about something that is beside the point. Its moral applies universally, but perhaps most incisively in diplomatic and bureaucratic circles.

THE LEAVES AND THE ROOTS
IVAN KRYLOV

It was a lovely summer's day
Casting its shadow along the valley.
The leaves on a tree were whispering to the gentle breezes
Blabbing on to those breezes
Bragging about their green riches:
"Don't you agree that our beauty dominates the valley
That a tree can be so lush and luxuriant, so magnificent and
majestic
Only thanks to us?
Where would a tree be without us leaves? No, it's true.
Let's face it: We've every right
To praise ourselves to the high heavens.
Do we not provide cool shelter in our shade
To the shepherd and the pilgrim?
Do we not, in all our beauty, entice the shepherdesses
To do their dances below us?
Is it not from our midst that the nightingale's crescendo
Sails out into the dusk and dawn?
And you, gentle breezes, you barely ever part with us."
But then a meek and humble voice replied
From under the earth.
"You could, at least, express some thanks to us."
"Who dares speak so insolently and impudently?!
Who are you down there

To speak with such impertinence to us?"
Blurted out the leaves, rustling noisily.
The answer came from below.
"We are the ones here digging in the dark.
We feed and nourish you … don't you know that?
We are the roots of the tree on which you thrive.
Flourish in your beauty, in all good time!
But bear in mind the difference between you and us …
Every spring brings new leaves into life.
But if a root so much as withers, dying away
There'd be no tree, let alone any leaves upon it."

During the nine months that I read these poems on my YouTube channel, there were many that I felt had significance for the trials that people all around the world were going through. But no poem spoke more eloquently about the unsung heroes working in our clinics and hospitals than "The Leaves and the Roots." Where would we have been without those who nourished us in body and mind?

Poems from Polish

BOLESŁAW LEŚMIAN (1877-1937) was a Polish poet who wrote ballads, lyrical fables and erotic poems. His poetry can be seen as a kind of dialogue with God about the meaning of sensuality and love. The descriptions of nature, inspired by his childhood spent in Ukraine, are exquisite. (His father worked for the Southwestern Kiev Railways.) Long after his death, his writing became popular, particularly from the time of the liberal literary policies of the 1960s. Many of his poems have been turned into songs sung by famous performers such as Ewa Demarczyk and Krystyna Janda. Julian Tuwin (see page 111) called him "the Ambassador on Earth of the Land of Poetry."

He is close in some ways to the renowned playwright, poet and painter of the "Young Poland" movement Stanisław Wyspiański, who depicted a folkloric Poland and wrote that the real Poland was heard in the beating of the heart. The artists and writers of Young Poland, a movement that dominated Polish arts in the last decade of the nineteenth century and the first two of the twentieth, created works rich in neo-Romantic ideas and symbolist images. It was, in a word, a kind of Polish nation-affirming art nouveau.

Leśmian (pronounced LESH-me-an) was great friends with Balmont. They had met in the Luxembourg Gardens in Paris in 1905. Balmont was so taken with Leśmian's poetry that he offered to pay him a rouble for each poem. (Where poor Balmont got the money I don't know.) Leśmian was so encouraged that he wrote poems in Russian. The poet that Leśmian is closest to in style—experimental, empirical, intimately impassioned—is Andrei Bely.

One of his great loves was Dora Lebenthal, a gynecologist from Warsaw to whom he wrote in a letter, "I lick the dirt from your scented feet and curls." He wrote the erotic poem "In a Raspberry Thicket" under her spell in 1917. (His wife Zofia insisted on a divorce and Leśmian said he would kill himself if she went through with it, so she desisted.) In the poem he is picking raspberries with Dora, and when her fingers are soaked in their juice, like blood, he greedily devours the fruit from her hand.

Leśmian was so obsessed by love and concerned about his prowess that he flirted with the prospect of having an operation devised by the Russian French surgeon Serge Voronoff in which the testicles of a monkey are grafted onto those of a man. Fortunately Leśmian decided to stick with his own testicles in the end.

Nobel laureate Czesław Miłosz famously remarked on Leśmian's often bizarre and innovative many-layered poetic language that it was "almost untranslatable," and I couldn't let such a thing stand. I have two remarkable Polish teachers, both Leśmian scholars, to thank again and again: Rochelle Stone, whose beginning Polish class I attended at UCLA in 1965; and Jacek Trznadel, who lectured on Leśmian at the Sorbonne when I was there in the spring of 1967. Both wrote ground-breaking books about him.

During Leśmian's lifetime the Polish literary establishment harassed him, at least partially due to his Jewish origins; and though he was finally elected to the Polish Academy at the end of his life, they left his body unburied for some time as a kind of official posthumous snub.

British actor Gillian Hills, who has appeared in classic films such as "Blow Up" and "A Clockwork Orange," is Leśmian's granddaughter.

IF I MET YOU AGAIN FOR THE FIRST TIME
BOLESŁAW LEŚMIAN

If I met you again for the first time
But in some other garden, in some other wood
The trees might echo differently for us
Stretching, boundless, into their mists

Maybe your palms would chill and shudder
Amidst the green rills of other flowers
Maybe some other words would slip
From obtuse lips … any other words

Maybe even the sun would enslave us
Until our soul rolled into a cascade of roses …
If I met you again for the first time
But in some other garden, in some other wood

"If I Met You Again for the First Time" is a love song set in a garden. The metaphor of the sun enslaving the lovers is telling. The Polish verb here is *zniewolić*, which means "to deprive of one's freedom" and also "to enthrall." This speaks of a possessive bond of love that counters the ifs and the maybes in the poem.

KONSTANTY ILDEFONS GAŁCZYŃSKI (1905-1953) was a celebrated poet, dramatist and satirist. His skits for the "Green Goose Theater" were legendary in his time. He spent four years of his youth (1914-1918) in Moscow, where he began writing poetry. In 1930 he married Natalia Awałow, author and translator of Russian literature (she was of Georgian and Russian origin and translated Chekhov and Gorky, among others). Cosmopolitan and well traveled, Gałczyński served in the culture department in the consular section of the Polish Embassy in Berlin from 1931 to 1933, after which he lived in Vilnius, where he certainly fell under the spell of the Romantic poets of Polish Lithuania, Adam Mickiewicz in particular (see page 117).

Gałczyński (pronounced Gao-CHIN-ski) returned to Warsaw in 1936 and was subsequently drafted into the army and mobilized on 24 August 1939. But on 17 September he was captured by the Germans and transported to Stalag XI-A outside the village of Altengrabow about ninety kilometers southwest of Berlin. The camp housed tens of thousands of prisoners from Poland, Russia, France, Britain, the US, Australia and other countries. (Another famous POW beside Gałczyński was Maurice Chevalier, who was also taken prisoner in the first weeks of the war. Chevalier spent only two years there before being released thanks to the intervention of King Alfonso XIII of Spain.) Gałczyński didn't immediately return to Poland after the war, staying in Belgium, France and Holland. In 1946 he went back to Poland.

It was in that year that he began writing his sketches and skits for the "Green Goose Theater." These appeared on the last page of the very popular weekly magazine "Przekrój." (While living in Warsaw and Krakow in 1966 I read it religiously.) In these hilarious vignettes he sent up Poland and the Poles with biting, often absurd, wit. That this was popular in the last years of Stalin's repression was a tribute to Gałczyński's brilliance, though the run ended in 1950, three years before his and Stalin's death.

His popularity continued to grow after his death from a heart attack (his third). The Polish government has issued both commemorative coins and a stamp in his name.

His wife Natalia died in Warsaw in 1976 and is buried there with her husband. All five of their grandchildren presently live in Australia. One of his granddaughters, Gabrisha, contacted me after she watched the reading of her grandfather's poems on "Roger Pulvers Reads." She informed me that her father Konstantin had passed away just two weeks before the reading.

A LYRICAL EXCHANGE
KONSTANTY ILDEFONS GAŁCZYŃSKI

Tell me the ways you love me.

I will.

Well then?

I love you in the sun. And in flashes of candlelight.
I love you in a hat and in your beret.
In a gust of wind on an avenue, and at the concert.
Amidst the lilacs, the birches, the raspberries, the maples.
And when you sleep. And when you're lost to work.
And when you elegantly crack an egg …
Even if the spoon slips from your fingers.
In a cab. In a car. There are no exceptions.
At the end of a street. At the beginning of a street.
And when you're parting your hair with a comb.
When you're in danger. And on the carousel.
At sea. In the mountains. In galoshes. In bare feet.
Today. Yesterday. And tomorrow. Day and night.
And when the swallow arrives in the spring.

And how do you love me in the summer?

Burning.

And in the autumn, with its clouds and caprices?

Even then, when you lose umbrellas.

And in the winter, with its silvery window frames?

In the winter I love you like holiday flames.
Next to your heart. Touching your heart.
It's snowing out the window.
And on that snow sit crows.

"A Lyrical Exchange" features a *rozmowa*, or conversation, between lovers. Its beauty lies in its simplicity. There are no flights of symbolism or ethereal references here. Its essential objects are everyday items: a hat, an egg, a spoon, a comb, galoshes…. This is a dialogue between two people who know each other well and love each other deeply, though the image at the very end leaves something hanging.

MOON DUST

KONSTANTY ILDEFONS GAŁCZYŃSKI

I long to be moon dust under your feet
The wind through your ribbon, the milk in your cup
A cigarette between your lips
A footpath among the cornflowers
A bench where you lie, a book that you read

To stitch through you like thread, to surround you like space
To be the season that your eyes adore
The fire in your hearth, and the roof that protects you
From the rain.

"Moon Dust," written in 1946, is another beautiful love song, where the down-to-earth imagery of objects contrasts with the title.

WHY DOESN'T A PICKLE SING?
KONSTANTY ILDEFONS GAŁCZYŃSKI

The question posed by this title
Is put so daringly
That it must be tackled
No matter how great the pain.

If a pickle doesn't sing
I mean, at the drop of a hat
It may very well mean
That Heaven forbids it.

But what if it longs to, passionately
Like no one's longed before, like a lark
Shedding tears
Into the jar of night?

Years fly by, winters come and go.
Now there's a spot of sunshine, now a little cloud.
And we pass right on before pickles
As if they weren't there at all.

"Why Doesn't a Pickle Sing" is a good example of Gałczyński's absurd sense of humor as seen in the "Green Goose Theater." And yet, there definitely seems to be a serious message lurking behind the nonsense, about people not noticing the wonderful things around them. I love the theatricality of this poem.

HORSE AT THE THEATER
KONSTANTY ILDEFONS GAŁCZYŃSKI

Through an oversight a horse was invited
   to the dress rehearsal of a certain satirical play:
"That it would be an honor, etc.
That the seats would be the best."
The horse arrived a trifle late, to make
   the so-called grand entrance.

At first the ushers didn't want to admit him
   yet spoke one usher to the other:
"It's not worth losing sleep over, I mean
   we'd better let him in, 'cause
   he's got the mane and the neigh …
But what if he's not a somebody?"
"At a glance I'd say it's a horse too.
But at the bottom it might be a VIP.
Life is full of appearances, and on
   appearances alone a guy
   might hold back a horse or a rabbit
   with the most unpleasant consequences!"
So, then and there, they bowed low.

The horse found himself at the theater.
He passed before the front row to show that he
   was "actively and so forth."
Throughout the entire performance he stood
   with his head rotated toward the audience.

Someone sang a song, and he stood
  (with one hoof on the railing)
distributing the compliments, each performer
  getting their due, now heartfelt, now faint
as Lucretius would have said:
"May all people get what's coming to them."

During the intermission several editors
  cornered him about a poem (viz. "Indonesia")
seeing as the horse had mastered in no time
  the term "Concept"
propagating it with every step
  even adding "Aspect."
The Heeheehee Concept. The Heeheehee Aspect.

Someone snapped his photo. Someone shot him
for a movie, since, what're we talkin' about …
a horse is a sensation.
And for the finale, there was grass
  painted on stage.
The horse leapt. And devoured the grass, getting
  the noisiest bravos.

In "Horse at the Theater" the drama occurs in the audience, where VIPs take up the best seats and prance around like stars. Of course, this being 1953, when the poem was written, the audience ("the people of Poland") give these prominent personages their public approval. They have little choice in the matter. I published this translation in "The Australian," the national daily newspaper, in 1976.

MARIA PAWLIKOWSKA-JASNORZEWSKA (1891-1945) was a poet, playwright and active champion of women's rights of the interwar period. She associated with the Skamander poets, such as Julian Tuwim and the artist-playwright-novelist Witkiewicz (whose plays I have, for over fifty years, concentrated my Polish studies on, translated and directed). Witkiewciz's portrait shows her with tears rolling down her cheeks. Her own plays, some for radio, are predominantly comedies, but they take up issues like illicit affairs, abortion and incest in a way far ahead of their time. Her take on motherhood was not altogether positive, but this can be seen in light of her belief that a woman had the total right to control her own life. Her final play sent up totalitarian regimes with a focus on the Nazis. It opened in Warsaw on 2 September 1939, the day after the Nazi invasion of her country. Her husband Stefan and she left Poland immediately and never returned.

Pawlikowska-Jasnorzewska (pronounced Pav-lee-KOV-ska Ya-sno-ZHEV-ska) married three times and enjoyed numerous lovers. But her great love was her husband Stefan, who was a captain in the Polish Airforce (she had a soft spot for flyers, one of whom, a Portugese named Manuel Sarmento de Beires, had completed a flight across the Atlantic). She and Stefan traveled extensively in their time together, mainly in France, Greece, Italy, Turkey and all the way to Africa. When they escaped Poland in 1939, they managed to reach London. From there they went to Blackpool, where Stefan was stationed at the RAF center. He was transferred around Britain and they were separated but corresponded with each other. Some of her letters were published recently in a volume titled *With Only You*.

Stefan was at her bedside when she died on 9 July 1945 in Manchester, this woman about whom he had written to his family back in 1932, "I have discovered a magnificent and exotic flower and I will never leave her." Stefan died thirty-five years after she died, and they are buried together in Southern Cemetery in Manchester.

In her poetry she is like Marina Tsvetaeva and Sylvia Plath: direct, affirmative of her feelings and full of sensuality. In "A Photograph" she sings of the "once-in-a-blue-moon bliss." She had more than her share of such rare bliss and shared it with us in her white-hot verse.

DIP ME IN HIM

MARIA PAWLIKOWSKA-JASNORZEWSKA

Dip me in him
Like a rose in a jug
Up to my eyes
To my forehead
To the trusses of my fairest hair.
Let him swim around me
Let him undulate through me
Like the waters of the Pacific Ocean
Caressing me.
Let the night and the dawn vanish
Let the glare of the moon and the sun die out
So long as he pierces me
Like violin music.
And when that reaches my heart
I will be his sweetest
Part.

"Dip Me in Him," written in 1922, is a poem brimming with erotic metaphors ("a rose in a jug," "undulating water"). She is clearly desiring to lose herself in her lover until, oblivious of the moon and the sun, they reach total fulfilment together.

THE MAN WHO WANTS ME TO LOVE HIM
MARIA PAWLIKOWSKA-JASNORZEWSKA

The man who wants me to love him
Must never be somber or glum
And he must manage to lift me as high as the sky.

The man who wants me to love him
Must be able to sit on a bench
And scrutinize the worms and every tiny blade of grass.

And he must yawn when the funeral procession passes
And the God-fearing masses howl before him.

But he must also be suitably moved
When, for instance, a cuckoo cuckoos
Or a woodpecker pecks persistently
On a beech tree's silver skin.

He must know how to pet and fondle a dog
And how to pet and fondle me as well
And how to laugh and in the end
Live the sweetest vacant dreams

And being ignorant of everything
As I am ignorant of everything
Remain in luxurious darkness

Without saying a word
And be as remote from evil
As he is from good.

"The Man Who Wants Me to Love Him," written in 1924, paints the portrait of a woman who gets readily bored with a banal partner. And he's got to be a skilled lover as well. Yet, within all this there is the silence of "luxurious darkness." It is there, where there is no need for words, that the line between evil and good vanishes.

JULIAN TUWIM (1894-1953) was a prolific and popular poet, librettist and lyricist of the interwar period. He translated many works into Polish from German, French, Russian and Latin. Even today many Polish children still read and love the poems he wrote for them. He met author and translator Stefania Marchew in 1912 and four years later they went to live in Warsaw, marrying in 1919. Throughout his years in Warsaw Tuwim was very active as a journalist, publishing in leading weeklies and monthlies, and as a writer for cabarets.

Being Jewish, Tuwim (pronounced TOO-veem) decided that it was wise to emigrate, moving with his wife to Romania and France, then Portugal and Brazil. In 1942 the Tuwims traveled from Brazil to New York, where he worked and wrote for "Nowa Polska" (New Poland), a monthly published in London.

The Tuwims returned to Poland in 1946, from which time he published poems in popular magazines. He also served as artistic director of the Nowy Theater in 1948 and 1949, remaining there as chief dramaturg until 1951. In 1949 he published what became his most famous work, the epic poem "Polish Flowers."

Among his poems is one that flaunts today's cancel culture. I wanted to include it in my Youtube readings but thought it—though I adore it—a trifle too profane for the Year of Covid. Its title is "All of You Can Kiss My Ass" and in it Tuwim writes, in part ...

> *Tiresome scowling Socialists*
> *Liberals and neo-Catholics*
> *Eager jumpers for culture*
> *Devotees of the radio and physics*
>
> *...*
>
> *Learned apes, wiseacres so crass*
> *All of you can kiss my ass!*

He is an equal opportunity abuser in this poem, including in those he implores to unite their lips with his backside: coal miners, doctors, intellectuals, pedagogues at girls' schools, Zionists, Pan-Slavic dreamers, and "medalists of the sporty class/All of you can kiss my ass!"

I do love this poem and look forward to the day when it will be publishable again.

Tuwim suffered from agoraphobia and severe depression, falling into alcoholism when he felt he was losing control. He died on 27 December 1953 after a heart attack. Stefania died in 1991 and is buried together with her husband in the same cemetery where the Gałczyńskis lie.

In his poem "My Wife" he recognizes how difficult it must be for Stefania to live with him. He writes from her standpoint about himself…

> *My husband is a nitwit, a spendthrift, a slacker*
> *He's either loitering by the window*
> *Or skirting around town all day long.*
> *…*
> *He quaffs vodka in the evening. I get cross.*
> *His darling eyes cloud over*
> *In a drunken mist.*

Witkiewicz drew two wonderful pastel portraits of the Tuwims that can be seen on the internet.

TO THE COMMON MAN

JULIAN TUWIM

When notices once again begin to appear
Posted with fresh glue on walls
And when the dreaded black print strikes:
"To Our People" … "To Our Soldiers!"
And every lout and every pipsqueak
Believes in those eternal lies
That you've got to go and take up arms
Murder, loot, poison, burn …
When for the thousandth time they begin
To yank up the Homeland
And to deceive with colorful mottos
And roll out "historical grounds"
Of time spans, glory and borders
Of fathers, ancestors and flags
Of heroes and of victims …
When out come the bishop, the pastor and the rabbi
To bless your rifles, and the Good Lord Himself
Has whispered to them from a great height
That we all must fight for the homeland …
When the shrill type of front pages
Screams out bent signals
And a herd of wild old women
Begins to heap flowers on our "dear soldiers" …
Oh, my ill-informed friend, my fellow man

From this or any other land!
Know that kings flanked by blimp-like lords
Are ringing the bells with alarm.
Know that they're pulling the wool over your eyes
When they shout in your face: "Shoulder arms!"
That they have land that gushes oil
Yielding barrels overflowing with dollars
That they don't deal with the usual banks
That they've smelled out fuller coffers elsewhere
Or tracked down fatter cats who'll cross
Their dripping palms with duties.
So spill your fucking bullets on the pavement!
It's your blood for their oil!
And from one capital to another
Cry out, protecting yourself and your muscle:
"We're not your fall guys, my dear overlords!"

"To the Common Man" is one of the world's most powerful pacifistic poems, on a par, to my mind, with Boris Vian's "Le déserteur" (The Deserter). Tuwim said, "I address in this poem all nations." It was first published on 27 October 1929 in the "Robotnik" (Worker), a Warsaw daily. From that day Tuwim incurred the wrath of those right-wing authoritarians who fancy themselves patriots. The editor-in-chief of Robotnik faced criminal charges over its publication. Some Polish fascists came out in the open suggesting that Tuwim be hanged for suggesting that Polish soldiers should consider desertion. Not much has changed in the world since 1929.

The language of the poem is typical Tuwim in its range of registers ("pipsqueaks" to "heroes," and "fat cats" to "dear soldiers"); and in its messages he pulls no punches: It is clear that the true enemies of the people are the capitalists and their apologists dressed in top hats and religious robes. The verb "spill" used in the imperative mood in the fifth line from the bottom can also mean "fuck" in Polish, hence the modifier for bullets.

MIRACLES AND WONDERS
JULIAN TUWIM

One day in July
A light-blue snow
Fell out of the sky.
Little birds barked
As dogs twittered and chirped.
Cows flew across
Azure meadows and fields
As the little green sun
Sang high in the sky.
Tiny butterflies knitted nests
On the petals of flowers.
And it all took place in two blinks of an eye.
I gazed up at that awesome realm
With my two eyes
Shut tight to the light.
When I opened them up
It had all disappeared
And the world went back
To the way it was.
Everything flows
A beautiful sight.
So from time to time
I'm going to keep
My eyes shut tight.

I suppose that "Miracles and Wonders" comes within the category of poems for children, but its charming paradoxes and spectacular imagery make for a world in which "Everything flows/A beautiful sight." It is a call to adults to retain a child's imagination in order to see this dreamlike world of ours.

ADAM MICKIEWICZ (1798-1855) was a poet, playwright and political activist. He is to Poland what Goethe is to Germany, Dante to Italy and Shakespeare to Britain. But in a sense his presence in the national narrative exceeds in importance that of those other icons of their nation.

By the time Mickiewicz was born, the Polish nation had been partitioned among Russia, Prussia and Austria and was not to be reborn until 1918. The ethos and very existence of the Polish nation itself was kept alive by its writers and artists. Every word, phrase and expression of the Polish language, every thread in fabric in the traditional Polish dress, Polish dances, Polish hairstyles, Polish food—the names of soups, stews, dumplings, mushrooms found in Polish forests—all continued to exist in the national consciousness as symbols of the nation thanks to poems, novels, plays and paintings. The opening words of what became the Polish national anthem, written in 1798, just two years after the Third Partition, affirm that "Poland is Not Yet Lost, So Long as We Still Live." It may just as well have read, "Poland is Not Yet Lost, So Long as Our Culture Still Lives."

Adam Mickiewicz (pronounced Mits-K'AY-vich) became the premier spokesperson of that culture. In addition, he fought for Polish independence in clandestine organizations, was exiled within Russia for five years, then continued the struggle to keep the Polish national identity alive throughout Europe (where, in Weimar, he befriended Goethe).

Mickiewicz's two great dramatic works are "Forefathers' Eve" and "Pan Tadeusz," the latter of which was made into a film in 1999 by Andrzej Wajda. But it is "Forefathers' Eve" (titled "Dziady" in the original) that has captured the imagination of Poles for nearly two centuries. The play revolves around a traditional feast commemorating the dead (*Dziady*, pronounced JA-dee, here means "forefathers"). It is a masterpiece of Romantic folklore, apart from its astounding literary value, taking up themes of love, wisdom and salvation.

"Forefathers' Eve" has had many epic productions in Poland,

productions that have had political as well as artistic significance. Artist, poet and playwright Stanisław Wyspiański directed it in 1901 in Krakow; Leon Schiller, in 1934 in Warsaw (the production by Schiller was remounted in 1948 but was not allowed to open due to ukase from the Kremlin: a Poland that is "too independent" is seen as a threat to paranoid Russians); and Kazimierz Dejmek staged the play in 1967 at the National Theater in Warsaw. Dejmek's production triggered events that proved to be of national and international importance.

Mickiewicz had written the critical introduction to the third part of "Forefathers' Eve" in 1832, while he was in Dresden. He openly dedicates the play to the Polish martyrs who died at the hands of their Russian oppressors. In Dejmek's production the prison scenes begin with the appearance of a fiery-red banner, a symbol of Polish martyrdom. Read red for blood. When the hero, played by the wonderful actor Gustaw Holoubek, stepped downstage in chains, members of the audience shouted that the chains must be undone. The government could not let this stand. On 21 December 1967, after only a few performances, the Central Committee and Ministry of Culture informed Dejmek that his production was "anti-Russian, anti-Soviet and anti-religion" (as for the first two "antis," it certainly was). First Secretary Władysław Gomułka, who had been a prisoner of the Soviets himself and was considered a mild liberal, stated that the production was "a stab in the back of Polish-Soviet friendship" (which is most certainly was as well). The production was closed down on 1 February 1968. After the last performance a large crowd left the theater and paraded to the Adam Mickiewicz monument in the center of the city shouting, "Free art! Free theater!" Thirty-five of the protesters were arrested for "creating a public disturbance." Demonstrations and petitions followed in the ensuing weeks, leading to further widespread political protests. The government response was a crackdown on artistic freedom and a wave of political oppression and anti-Semitism (the go-to place for crackdowns), not to mention a mass purge in the Party and the emigration of more than 15,000 Jews, among them two of my closest friends, Janina Katz and Ryszard Taedling, both of whom went on to Denmark and created successful careers in the arts and journalism.

This is the role that Adam Mickiewicz has played—and continues to play—in his native Poland.

AMBIVALENCE

ADAM MICKIEWICZ

When you are not before my eyes I do not sigh, I do not cry
And when I catch sight of you I do not lose all sense
But when for ages you have not appeared before me
I am somehow incomplete. I need to see … someone
And languishing like that I ask myself this question:
Is this friendship? Or am I in love?

When you vanish from my sight
Your image fades away in my mind's eye
And yet, in spite of all desire
It lingers constantly on the edge of memory
And I repeat the question to myself:
Is this friendship? Or am I in love?

I have suffered ceaselessly and yet have never wished
To burden you with sorrowful self-pity
I have roamed around not caring where I went
And do not know how I found myself on your doorstep
But once there I ask myself this question:
What led me here … friendship or love?

I would offer my life to keep you well
I would descend to Hell to give you peace
And though I am lacking in bold passion and desire

I would do anything for your safety and well-being
So once again I ask myself this question:
Is this friendship? Or am I in love?

When you put your hand on my palm
I feel enwrapped in tranquillity
As if my life were about to end in a light and easy sleep
And yet my heart is awakened and it beats with life
Asking me this question aloud:
Is this friendship? Or is it also love?

When I composed this little song for you
It was not the poet's spirit that moved my lips
I myself was surprised, astonished …
Where did I find these thoughts, these lyrics?
And at the end I wrote down a question:
What was inspiring me … is it friendship or is it love?

"Ambivalence" (literally from the Polish word for "uncertainty"), one of Mickiewicz's most famous poems, is a soliloquy or internal monologue, a confession of strong feelings that the hero cannot identify in just one word. It was published in the late 1820s in his collection "Odessan Sonnets." While in Odessa he had fallen in love with his friend's sister, Karolina. The friend was Henryk Rzewuski, Polish nobleman and writer (they had traveled together to the Crimean Peninsula and later met up in Rome; it is thought that Rzewuski's stories about Polish traditions in the nobility spurred Mickiewicz to write "Pan Tadeusz"). But Karolina did not requite his love and he turned his attentions to one of her friends, Joanna, who actually fell for him. He attempted, however, to find out how Karolina felt about him from her. No wonder, then, that he is riven by doubts over his own feelings. In the end he equates these doubts—this ambivalence—to the creative process itself.

MARIA KONOPNICKA (1842-1910) was a poet, author of novels and books for children, translator and journalist. She was born in the little northeastern Polish town of Suwałki, coincidentally the hometown of film director Andrzej Wajda. A vitally important event occurred in 1863, when she was twenty. Her brother Jan was killed in the January Uprising against the Russian occupiers. Later she herself would become an anti-imperial activist.

Konopnicka (pronounced Ko-nop-NITS-ka) began publishing her poetry in 1870. Some of it is lyrical to the point of being melodic, while other poems, such as "There, in My Country," are virtual calls-to-arms. One of my favorite poems of hers is like a rhapsody, and I fell in love with and memorized it when I lived in Poland in 1966. It begins like this …

> *I would go to the ends of the earth*
> *Like the wind that flies over a field*
> *Like the wind that drives the clouds*
> *White clouds, swan-down clouds*
> *Into the grim dark distance*
> *Only … I pity you, you the earth*

Konopnicka was a committed campaigner for women's and children's rights. (There is a lovely monument to her in the Saski Garden in Warsaw. It was erected at the initiative of the children of the city of Kalisz and unveiled in 1966. I went there on my last visit to Warsaw in April 2019, stood before the statue and recited the above poem to myself.) Her summer home, an eighteenth-century manor house in Zarnowiec, a village near Jedlicze in the southeast corner of Poland, is now a museum dedicated to her life and work. Two of her daughters, Laura and Zofia, are buried there.

THERE, IN MY COUNTRY
MARIA KONOPNICKA

There, in my country so far, far away
A hundred extinguished stars form a crown
A hundred extinguished stars standing over a field
Like a hundred knights in the armor of iron

There, in my country so far, far away
A hundred ardent hearts burn with longing
A hundred ardent hearts beat in the breast
Like a spirit forged in the iron of armor

There, in my country so far, far away
A hundred gales beat across the vast pasture
A hundred gales strike grassland trails
Like golden horseshoes on a hundred horses

After the passing of one hundred days and one hundred nights
The knights will arise with the force of life in their hearts
The knights will arise, they will mount those horses
And set fire to that crown of golden stars

"There, in My Country" was published in 1915, five years after her death and three years before Poland regained its independence. It urges courage and fortitude in harking back to a time that Poland was free ("my country so far, far away"). It recalls the Legend of the Sleeping Knights of Giewont. The legend tells of a blacksmith from the town of Zakopane in the Tatra Mountains who saw an army of knights asleep next to their armor and helmets. The blacksmith had been asked by a stranger to make a horseshoe out of gold and shoe one of the knight's horses with it. The blacksmith learns that the knights had been there in a deep sleep for centuries and would only wake to fight a great battle … to claim victory for Poland.

Giewont, a mountain massif 1,894 meters tall and 2.7 kilometers long in the Tatras, resembles in its northern profile a sleeping knight. Witkiewicz's father, among other artists, famously painted the mountain; and Witkiewicz himself photographed it beautifully from the porch of the family home in Zakopane. In "There, in My Country" Konopnicka sings that the brave knights of Poland's present will bring the stars back to the Polish sky.

TADEUSZ BOROWSKI (1922-1951) was a poet, author and journalist. He was born in Zhytomyr, a city in northwest Ukraine. Both of his parents were deported to different parts of the USSR. By the time his mother returned he was twelve. His father was forced to work on the White Sea Canal; his mother had found herself in Siberia.

Borowski (pronounced Bo-ROV-ski) enrolled clandestinely in the banned Faculty of Polish Literature at Warsaw University in 1940. It was at this time that he met and fell in love with Maria Rundo, whom he described in poems and his short story collection, *Farewell to Maria*. But in late February 1943 he was arrested and sent, via the notorious Pawiak Prison, to Auschwitz, where his number was 119198. In late 1944 he was transferred to Allach, an external camp of Dachau and was liberated on 1 May 1945 by the US Seventh Army's Forty-fifth Infantry Division just days before the war ended. He was sent to a DP camp at Freimann, not far from Munich and began working for the Polish Red Cross. His main goal was to find Maria, who had been arrested by the Gestapo and sent from one German camp to another and, after the war, had entered a sanatorium in Sweden.

Borowski had continued to write even when in captivity. Among the stories that came out after the war was his classic, "This Way to the Gas, Ladies and Gentlemen." These stories were not viewed favorably by the Catholic church and the Communist government, and Borowski was forced to turn to journalism and write what was essentially propagandistic pap.

He and Maria married after her return to Warsaw in November 1946. But the postwar years saw him make a stark turnaround. He became a member of the Polish Workers' Party and worked in military intelligence in both Warsaw and East Berlin. A daughter, Małgorzata, was born to them on 26 June 1951, but a few days after the birth he turned on the gas and took his own life, dying on 3 July. He was twenty-nine years old. (Małgorzata became a professor of philology at the University of Warsaw.)

His story "The Battle of Grunwald" was adapted for the screen by

Andrzej Wajda under the title "Landscape after the Battle." The hero is a poet named Tadeusz who experiences severe PTSD from having been a prisoner in a concentration camp, the scene of the story and film. This is a love story between him and a Polish Jewish girl named Nina. (This film was made in the year I met Andrzej Wajda, 1970, and it had an inordinately profound effect on me, inspiring, in part, the novel *Star Sand* that I wrote and made into a film many years later.)

Borowski's poems are full of suffering, longing and—despite all the brutality that he lived through—tender love. On 3 August 1945 he wrote to his family from the DP camp, "My dears, I survived the war." But, in actuality, he didn't. He had predicted correctly when he wrote to his mother in January 1944, long before liberation, "I'm just a bit tired and I fear that I will never be the same as I was before."

I AM THINKING OF YOU

TADEUSZ BOROWSKI

I am thinking of you. I look up
At the sky and recall your eyes
Your voice and the smile on your lips.
A cloud is gliding down
The sloping sky, like you
When you turn your profile
Lightly to the left. Here a tree
Entangled in the wind inclines
As you do when you bow.
There a bird is hanging in the air
And I know that's how your palm
Is still against your face
When you're plunged in thought.
The beauty of matter is scattered.
Yet, I know, its short-lived earthly flash
Has stuck to you, taking on
An actual and tangible shape.

Poems from Japanese

YOSANO AKIKO (1878-1942), poet, author and activist, played a crucial role in the formation of Japanese cultural and social life in the first four decades of the twentieth century. A great deal has been written about Yosano Akiko's life and poetry, which are, in any case, tightly intertwined. She was and is the greatest female poet of modern Japan.

Yosano Akiko was born in 1878 in Sakai, an old trading town in Osaka prefecture, where her father owned and ran a confectionary store. Writing poetry from an early age, she submitted some of her work to the new magazine, "Myojo," edited by poet Yosano Tekkan (the magazine lasted only eight and a half years, folding in 1908, but it was by far the most influential journal of Japanese poetry then and, perhaps, to this day). She met Tekkan in 1900; and though he was carrying on affairs with his former wife and one of Akiko's closest friends, the poet Yamakawa Tomiko, Akiko fell hopelessly in love with him. The two began living together the next year, 1901. (Yamakawa Tomiko, who was from Fukui prefecture on the Sea of Japan coast, died at the age of twenty-nine from the tuberculosis that she caught from her husband. There is a monument engraved with one of her tanka in Obama, the town she was born in.)

Yosano published more than twenty books of poetry in her lifetime, as well as a mass of social commentary in newspapers and periodicals, some of it openly opposed to Japan's aggressive policies, though toward the end of her life she advocated for the imperial cause. She died in 1942, when Japan's military was still able to celebrate a string of victories.

In going through the myriad details of her dramatic life that spanned the late-Meiji, Taisho and early-Showa eras, a dramatic fact stands out, to my mind, above all others: Yosano Akiko gave birth to thirteen children. This means that she was pregnant for about a decade of her adult life. It is hard to imagine her having the time to produce her vast output of poems and prose and letters—not to mention a translation of "The Tale of Genji" into modern Japanese—and to give birth to and look after eleven surviving children, admittedly with help from relatives and nannies, all the while catering to the many and complex whims of her very proud husband, whose fame as a poet she eclipsed.

Yosano primarily wrote tanka, a thirty-one-syllable traditional form of poetry, akin to a long haiku. She was a dedicated feminist in an era when most women were obliged to do the bidding of the men in their life. She fought for women to be financially independent from their family and partner. Her poetry is impassioned and openly erotic. As such, she is a pioneer of poetry written by women on the world stage. The tradition of female literature goes back as far as to the Heian period, when the two greatest literary classics, *The Tale of Genji* and *The Pillow Book* were both written by women who spoke openly about their deepest feelings and desires.

OH MY LITTLE BROTHER
YOSANO AKIKO

Oh my little brother I weep for you
Do not die, my little brother.
As their youngest child
You were bathed in our parents' love.
But did they teach you to hold a knife in your hand
So that you could murder men?
Did they bring you up to age twenty-four
To kill and to die?

Do not die, my little brother.
You carry the name of our family
The proud family of merchants
In the city of Sakai.
Who cares if the fortress of Lushun
Falls or not?
It is not the practice of merchants
To murder and be murdered.

Oh my little brother, do not die.
Would the Emperor in all his mercy
Keep out of battle himself
Then look upon as glorious
The spilling of blood
Into the beastly soil?

Oh my little brother, do not die
For this thing called "war."
Father passed away last fall
Leaving mother at home in mourning
Grieving for her son called to arms.
In this day of His Majesty's tranquil reign
Her hair turns white.

Have you forgotten your young bride
Weak, weeping in the half-shade of the shop door?
Is she in your thoughts?
Think of her tender heart
You who shared a bed with her
For a bare ten months.
She looks to you
You alone in the world.

My little brother … do not die.

In this day of menacing posturing and belligerency, it would be good to remember this passionate antiwar poem written about the Russo-Japanese War (1904-05), a war that enjoyed immense public support in Japan.

Akiko's little brother, Chusaburo, who was two years her junior, was a second lieutenant in the Imperial Army Reserve Eighth Infantry Regiment. Though, in fact, he may not have actually fought at Lushun, a strategic city whose English name at the time was Port Arthur, now a district of Dalian, he did serve in the Chinese theater. He returned to Japan after the war and lived a long life, dying two years after his sister, in 1944.

Akiko published "Oh My Little Brother" in the September 1904 issue of "Myojo." The poem naturally came in for much flak in that era of heady chauvinism. Despite today's drift toward saber rattling around the world, the culture of non-belligerency in Japan is alive and well. And it goes back a long way.

The following tanka are from "Disheveled Hair," the first volume of her tanka, containing some four hundred of them, published in 1901. The book took the Japanese literary world by storm. The very title is a symbol of passions unwound and left in ecstatic disarray.

TANKA FROM "DISHEVELED HAIR"
YOSANO AKIKO

Two stars are deep in heaven
Whispering love
Behind the nighttime curtain
While down below now people lie
Their hair in gentle disarray

Made to punish men for their sins
The smoothest skin
The longest black hair …
All that
Is me!

The day lengthens and I
Snap off wild roses, grasp
Them, put them in my hair …
I am weary of waiting in the field
For you!

I whisper to you "Stay in bed"
As I tenderly shake you awake
My disheveled hair now up
In a "butterfly" …
Kyoto morning!

My blood burns
To give you one night
In the shelter of dreams
God, do not look down on me
As I pass through spring

The words in the middle of this poem—*yoru no yume no yado* (a night in the shelter of dreams)—are among the most beautiful of any that she created. "Spring," of course, stands for young physical love. The Japanese word for "puberty" is *shishunki*, written with the characters for "think," "spring" and "time." Her tanka make one feel as if one were reading Heian poetry in a more modern form. In fact, for me this is one of the greatest modern tanka ever written. Had Yosano Akiko been writing in English or French or German, for instance, her influence on twentieth-century poetry around the world would have been immense.

I press my breasts
Gently parting
The shroud of mystery
Revealing the flower
Redder than red

"I press my breasts" is one of her most famous and most erotic tanka. With her poetry the associations are complex and varied: Heian poetry; haiku (particularly Buson and other classical haiku poets); tanka written by Tekkan and other contemporaries; elements of nature; and parts of the clothing or body. It is astounding how many of these elements are integrated into a single powerful image in so few words.

"Spring doesn't last," I said to him
"You don't believe in permanence, do you?"
And I took his hands in mine
Leading them
To my young full breasts

Tomorrow, this time tomorrow
You will not be with me …
I lean against the inn door, faint
As the plum blossoms darken
Before my eyes

Yesterday is another world
A thousand years away
Yet it rushes to me
This minute!
With your hand on my shoulder

What will come into my burning lips?
You answer …
"The blood from my little finger."
But that blood is too dry now
For my mouth

My skin is so soft
Fresh from my bath
It pains me to see it touched and covered
By the fabric
Of an everyday world

She loved European painting, especially the work of Titian. Is she picturing herself here just out of the bath in a Renaissance painting?

TERAYAMA SHUJI (1935-1983) was a playwright, theater and film director, and poet who played a central role in the postwar revival of avant-garde culture. He was born in the Tohoku castle town of Hirosaki, in Aomori prefecture. His father worked for the town police and was moved around a good deal. Perhaps this is why Terayama claimed that he was "born in a train and had no hometown." But he was notorious for making up spurious details about his childhood and upbringing. If you believed the confabulations in his self-styled autobiographical essays, you wouldn't be blamed for taking him to be a conglomerate of any number of bizarre characters in his dramas and films. He was essentially brought up singlehandedly by his mother. When she landed a job at an American base in Fukuoka prefecture, she left him with relatives in Aomori, some 1,200 kilometers by air from Fukuoka.

Terayama started writing tanka at a very early age and their quality was recognized by poet Tanikawa Shuntaro, among others. (Tanikawa became very close friends with him and ended up officiating at his funeral.) He was admitted into the prestigious private Waseda University. But illness got in the way of his studies. He suffered then and all his adult life from nephritic syndrome. He spent a year in bed in his late teens, a time, he said, that allowed him to read almost constantly. One of the books that had a great effect on him and his writing was Lautréamont's *The Songs of Maldoror*, the great prose-poem that became a bible for the Surrealists. Terayama was, essentially, a surrealist with his feet planted firmly on Japanese soil.

He founded his Tenjo Sajiki Theater in 1967. "Tenjo Sajiki" refers to the uppermost gallery, or gods, of a theater, and the reference came to Terayama from the French film "Les Enfants du Paradis." I first visited Tenjo Sajiki in March 1970, where I saw and was overwhelmed by his play "The Crimes of Dr. Garigari." The title is a pun on the title of the 1920 German experimental film "The Cabinet of Dr. Caligari." *Garigari* is a mimetic Japanese word that means "grate, rasp, crunch."

I met Terayama (and his mother!) in the little café that they ran adjacent to the stage; and though I saw him two times after that, both at premieres of his films, I regret that I never came to know him well.

Terayama's work was discovered by the outside world in the 1960s, and he took his plays to Europe. He had a genuinely big following there, particularly in France and Holland. In 2012 Tate Modern in Britain honored him with a showing of his films. His works still enjoy popularity in Japan, and there is a museum dedicated to him in Misawa in Aomori prefecture, where he lived as a child. His plays are still being performed, but not with the iconoclastic, chaotic and bombastic power of the productions that I saw between 1970 and the time of his death on 4 May 1983.

IF HAPPINESS WERE TOO FARAWAY
TERAYAMA SHUJI

If life were only
About goodbyes
   What would be the meaning of springs to come
   Or the meaning of the lilies in the meadows
   At the very ends of the Earth?

If life were only
About goodbyes
   What would be the meaning of meeting after separation
   Or the meaning of our love
   And the softest skies at sunset?

If life were only
About goodbyes
   What would be the meaning of the house we built
   Or the lights that shine
   On the vast empty plain?

If life is only
About goodbyes
I'll do without life

"If Happiness Were Too Faraway" is a love song. Despite the blast of nonnaturalistic imagery in Terayama's plays and films, there is an underlying sentimentality, naïve and often childlike, in them.

I KNOW NOTHING OF WAR
TERAYAMA SHUJI

I don't know the names of the flowers that bloom in the fields
But I love them nonetheless.
I can't hold back the tears that flow
While gathering flowers to fill my hat.

I don't know a thing about how people lived in the war
I don't have a father anymore.
When I think of him, the red sun … the red sun
Slips below the horizon above the wasteland.

Father, sorrowful father who fell in war
I am your daughter.
Twenty years have passed here in our hometown
And tomorrow I'm getting married.

Father so far away, please look upon me
Under this swift sky of cirrus clouds.
I have turned twenty without knowing war
I will be a bride, father, then a mother …
Father, I will be a mother.

I don't know the names of the flowers that bloom in the fields
But I love them nonetheless.

I can't hold back the tears that flow
While gathering flowers to fill my hat.

These are the words as they appear in the lyrics of the song as sung famously by Carmen Maki in her 1969 album, along with his version of "Sometimes I Feel like a Motherless Child." For Terayama, who experienced both the war and what it was like to survive it, "I Know Nothing of War" may very well have been the creation of his closest to his heart. In his version of "Sometimes I Feel like a Motherless Child" he writes …

Sometimes I just want to sit myself down
And write a long letter
Like a motherless child.
Sometimes I just want to scream
At the top of my lungs
Like a motherless child.
But I'd soon have a change of heart
If I did have no mother.
I couldn't speak of love … to anyone.
Sometimes I feel like a motherless child.

NAKAHARA CHUYA (1907-1937) was a poet known for his experimental style that he honed under the influence of French symbolist poets Rimbaud and Verlaine, both of whose work he translated. He is, to my mind, Japan's most painterly poet. If the ancient traditions of painting and poetry were united—many scrolls and pictures featured calligraphic poems written over them—then the same aesthetic elements of both come together in Nakahara's word pictures.

The great trauma of his life was the loss of his son, Fumiya, just after the little boy's second birthday in November 1936. Though another son, Yoshimasa, was born that month, Nakahara suffered a mental collapse and had to be hospitalized two months later. Yoshimasa also passed away in January 1938, three months after his father. His wife Takako was left alone and bereft.

During his lifetime, though he was never what you would call popular, Nakahara enjoyed the company and respect of many writers of his day, including novelist Ibuse Masuji (*Black Rain*), Ooka Shohei (*Fires on the Plain*), and the foremost literary critic of his time, Kobayashi Hideo. Nakahara may come across as a soft and sensitive fellow, but he was, in actuality, rather feisty. He got into a fight with Sakaguchi Ango (whose black-comic novel *In the Woods Beneath the Cherry Blossoms in Full Bloom* I have translated) at a bar in Ginza frequented by the literati. The fight was over a hostess, Sakamoto Mutsuko, who apparently was intimate with quite a few of the bar's high-brow customers. (Kobayashi Hideo asked her to marry him and she originally said yes, but later dumped him and ran off to Kyoto with an Olympic athlete.) The fight with the stouter Sakaguchi never really got off the ground, because when Nakahara put up his dukes in a showy manner, Sakaguchi just burst into laughter.

Nakahara died of cerebral meningitis at the age of thirty. Today he is considered one of Japan's greatest modern poets, and the Nakahara Chuya Prize is the country's leading award for poetry. He is buried in Yamaguchi, the city of his birth, where the Nakahara Chuya Memorial Museum is located.

THE POINT OF NO RETURN
NAKAHARA CHUYA

I found myself at the end of the world. Warm sunbeams streamed down, and flowers trembled in the wind.

All day long the dust on the wooden bridge fell silent … all day long the postbox flamed red … and the pram with the pinwheel seemed never to leave the street.

Not one of the resident adults or children was seen on the street, so I took it upon myself, having no next of kin there, to occasionally observe the color of the sky above the weathervane. And yet I was in no way bored. There was nectar in the air, and though that nectar wasn't solid, like food, it was just what the doctor ordered.

I did have a cigarette or two. Even so, it was more for the smell than for anything else, and on top of that I only smoked outdoors. Now, one towel was all the worldly goods that I possessed. I didn't even own anything resembling a pillow or what you would call a futon. I did boast a toothbrush, and my only book had nothing written in it, though I did get a kick out of weighing it in my palm, on the odd occasion.

As for women, I really did go for them, but I never felt moved to go out of my way to see one. I had enough of them in my dreams. Something I couldn't put my finger on kept urging me on, and my heart throbbed with hope, even though I had no purpose or end in view.

* * *

There was a truly weird park in the forest, where women and children and men were strolling, beaming with an eerie yet happy grin. I couldn't comprehend the language they were speaking or read their feelings from their faces.
That's when I caught sight of shiny silver spider webs gleaming in the sky.

"The Point of No Return" was published in November 1937, a month after his death. It is presumably set in Kyoto, where he visited as a middle school pupil. Naturally, the sights that he saw remained vividly within him. The bold contrast between the intangible—sunbeams, wind, sky—and the mundane—postbox, toothbrush, cigarette, towel—give this poem both a concrete and an ethereal quality rolled into one beautiful portrait of a day out. Just when he realizes that he is lost, not understanding language or facial expressions, he catches sight of great beauty—webs—linking the land with the sky.

A JUNE RAIN
NAKAHARA CHUYA

Once again there's a burst of rain
Morning rain, green as irises.
A calm and carefree woman
Her eyes glistening in tears
Appears, then vanishes
Into the thin air.

When she appears and vanishes
I am seized by grief
Like the drizzling rain
Falling and falling, ceaselessly
On a field.

The drums beat
And the flute sings out
While an innocent child plays games
At home on a Sunday.

And as he plays
The drums beat
And the flute sings out
And the rain keeps falling
On the other side
Of the slatted window.

"A June Rain" appeared in the June 1936 issue of "Bungakukai," a magazine that is still today the leading literary monthly. It won second place in the Bungakukai Prizes, losing out to a novel by Okamoto Kanoko (see page 156). This is no doubt a portrait written by an adoring father of his son, Fumiya. Outside the scene is serene, if gloomy, while inside, the child makes fun noises, as if to compete with the rain.

ONTO THE LAKE
NAKAHARA CHUYA

Let's take our boat out onto the lake
When the moon floats, bobbing in the sky.
Waves will be lapping against the shore
And gentle breezes will be blowing.

It will be dark by the time we're away.
The sound of water dripping off the oars
Will bring us closer to each other
As you pause, intermittently, in speaking to me.

The moon will slip a little lower
To listen intently to us
And be just above our heads
When our lips meet in a kiss.

Then you'll start to talk to me
Grumbling about this and that
And I will listen to your every word
As I row and row over the water.

So let's take our boat onto the lake
When the moon floats, bobbing in the sky.
Waves will be lapping against the shore
And gentle breezes will be blowing.

I must confess, I adore this poem. Japanese male poets are not generally known for their romantic verse, though there are exceptions. And "Onto the Lake" is one of them. Lines two and three feature the mimetic words "bobbing" and "lapping" that correspond to similar mimesis in Japanese, *pokkari* and *hitahita*. These are repeated in the last stanza. The water and the sky, with the lovers in between, are all part of a singular picture. "Onto the Lake" appeared in print in August 1930.

MIKI ROFU (1889-1964) was a poet and essayist best known for writing the poem that formed the lyrics of the song "Little Red Dragonfly." "Akatonbo," as it is called in Japanese, was voted the nation's "favorite song" in a nationwide survey conducted in 1989 by the popular NHK show *Nihon no Uta, Furusato no Uta* (Songs of Japan, Songs of our Hometowns).

He had decided on his profession while in secondary school, when he was already publishing his poems in journals and newspapers. He dropped out of school in his hometown of Tatsuno in Hyogo prefecture and went to Tokyo.

But the telling event in his childhood was the divorce of his parents when he was five and the departure of his mother from home. Miki associated the gathering of wild mulberries with this incident and waited at home, counting berries, thinking that his mother would step through the door at any time. His father was born into wealth but frittered much of it away on alcoholic binges that often lasted for days. His mother simply walked out with her younger son, Tsutomu, on her back and never returned. She subsequently went to the northern Hokkaido town of Otaru and, under the name Midorikawa Kata, became a magazine editor and early advocate of feminism. It wasn't until Miki was eighteen that he received a letter from her. He clutched the letter to him and wept.

Midorikawa Kata died in 1962 at the age of ninety-one. Carved on her white marble gravestone are the words "At rest here, little dragonfly's mother." Miki died only two years after her. He was seventy-five. He stepped out of a post office in Mitaka, Tokyo, and was struck by a taxi. He suffered a serious skull fracture and died in the hospital without regaining consciousness.

Miki Rofu's home in Tatsuno, a lovely small town on the Seto Inland Sea, is now a museum dedicated to his life and work.

LITTLE RED DRAGONFLY
MIKI ROFU

At sunset in the twilight's glow
Little red dragonfly …
Was it then that I caught sight of you
As a baby on my nanny's back?

Or am I dreaming this
Gathering wild mulberries
In that little basket
On the grasslands of the mountain?

The nanny wed at fifteen
And set out for a distant home
It wasn't long before letters ceased
To come to our hometown.

At sunset in the twilight's glow
Little red dragonfly …
Resting, waiting, stopped
On the end of a bamboo pole.

Although he refers to being on his nanny's back, it is clear that she is a poetic substitute for his mother, who married his father when she was fifteen. The image of the bamboo pole is a powerful one in Japan, where, even in the early years of my living there, itinerant salesmen would go from house to house shouting "Aodake … Aodake!" ("Green poles … Green poles!"). These bamboo poles were an outdoor feature of most every home, particularly in the countryside, the equivalent of the Western clothesline. The little red dragonfly perched on the end of the pole is, of course, the little boy himself, patiently waiting for his mother to come back home to him.

HAYASHI FUMIKO (1903-1951) was one of Japan's most popular novelists in the prewar and immediate postwar eras. Her father was a shady itinerant peddler who did not own up to his paternity of her. She spent her early childhood in Nagasaki, Sasebo, Shimonoseki and Kagoshima (her mother's hometown), among other cities, before moving to Onomichi, in Hiroshima prefecture at the age of thirteen. By eighteen she was writing prose and poetry for the local newspaper. The following year she followed a lover to Tokyo. In fact, perhaps fueled by her father's betrayal, Hayashi was a pioneering feminist who believed that women had just as much right as men to pursue their romantic interests as they saw fit. This became one of the recurring themes in her fiction as well.

In the capital, a series of tough menial jobs ensued, and for a time she was homeless. But in 1928 she began to publish, in what would be twenty installments, her novel *Horoki* (*The Diary of a Vagabond*), which came out as a book in 1930. This fascinating autobiographical novel became an instant hit, selling more than 500,000 copies. It has also been filmed three times, most famously by Naruse Mikio in 1962, with Tanaka Kinuyo in the lead.

Hayashi soon made a reputation for herself as a travel writer. In 1931 she went to Korea, then a colony of Japan, as well as to the USSR and France, before settling in London for a short while. She returned to Japan in the early summer of 1932.

The trip that started her on her journey as an embedded journalist with the imperial Japanese forces was one for the "Tokyo Nichi Nichi Shimbun" (today's "Mainichi Shimbun") in January 1938 to Nanjing (then Nanking), where her country's military had just brutally ravaged the population in what has come to be called the Nanking Massacre.

In 1940, Hayashi was again a trusted embedded reporter with Japanese forces in Manchuria and Korea. Then, for eight months in 1942 and 1943, she found herself in Vietnam, Singapore, Java and Borneo, all places under the control of Imperial Japan. Finally, in

1944, she returned to Japan and immediately evacuated with her elderly mother and her adopted toddler son to the remote hot springs village of Kanbayashi in Nagano prefecture.

Back in 1939, however, Hayashi had bought a plot of land in the Ochiai district of Tokyo's Shinjuku ward, where she had commissioned the architect Yamaguchi Bunzo to design a home for herself, her husband, mother and son. That was completed in 1941, but she didn't truly settle into life there until after the war. Immaculately preserved in every detail, including its lovely tranquil garden, the building is now the Hayashi Fumiko Memorial Hall, run as a museum by Shinjuku ward. It is one of my favorite places to visit in Tokyo and I have been there in all seasons.

Hayashi was never openly apologetic about her role in the war effort, though she had been the first Japanese woman of note to be in Nanjing after the massacre and the first to enter Hankow (present-day Wuhan) with the invading Japanese troops. So why, then, was she effectively exonerated by the public after the war?

She had joined the so-called Pen Corps and followed the troops. Her *Hokugan Butai* (*North Shore Corps*), describing life on the Chinese front, was published by Chuo Koron in 1939. There is next to nothing in it about the actual fighting. Rather it takes up, in documentary-like fashion, the routine personal trials of individual soldiers. Of course, this too, makes her an apologist for the war effort. But her personalized approach, nearly devoid of tactical details about battles, not only appealed to readers but also mitigated for a less vindictive attitude toward her once the war was over. In addition, I believe her sincere efforts to redeem herself through her fiction after the war is what saved her from what might have been an expected humiliation. She became a champion of the downtrodden victims of war, particularly women and children. She wrote tirelessly after the war about women who were victims of the war's brutality. In fact, after 1943, she had become disillusioned with the war effort and ceased to write about it. In Nagano, in 1944, she jotted this down: "I now see writing about reality today in the face of every obstacle and impediment as a personal sin in itself; and in this miserable country existence, unsupported and at wits' end, my only salvation is to write children's stories."

Under extreme pressure due to having taken on an overly heavy workload, Hayashi died of a heart attack in 1951 at the age of forty-seven. So many admirers crowded around the hearse carrying her body that the vehicle could not proceed for some time. Officiating at her funeral was novelist Kawabata Yasunari, who summed up her reputation succinctly: "The deceased often did terrible things to others in order to maintain her literary life," he said, "but in two or three hours, she will be reduced to ash. Death extinguishes all sin, so I ask you in your heart to forgive her."

In his play about the life of Hayashi, "Blow the Flute, Beat the Drums," Inoue Hisashi puts very telling words into the mouth of his heroine. I feel as if she could have said these words in real life, and that they represent a certain amount of redemption from her wartime sins. Perhaps the Japanese people who lived with her during the traumatic era sensed this too, which is why they forgave her and writers like her.

Inoue's Hayashi says: "I humble myself before the readers who danced to my flute and drums. Thanks to that flute and drums, there were war widows, there were soldiers who had to be repatriated, there were the orphans of war. And so, to show my deep and apologetic regret to my readers, I must write now about their suffering until my arm falls off, until my heart breaks in two …"

I have written extensively here about Hayashi Fumiko, a long prologue to a short poem. But I feel that her life, with its trials of poverty, rejection and rebirth as a committed feminist speaks loudly about the history of Japan's Showa era.

MY JOYOUS YOUTH

HAYASHI FUMIKO

My joyous youth is before me.
The colors of the sea in the distance
And the colors of the sky in the distance
Appear brilliant in my eyes today.
I love life!
I love being alive to breathe deeply
The breath of happiness.

Hayashi didn't exactly have what you would call "a joyous youth," but she certainly imagined a joyous life when she wrote "I don't want to live in the world as it is; I desire to go on new and exhilarating pilgrimages."

OKAMOTO KANOKO (1889-1939) was a novelist, poet and a leading feminist. She made her debut as a tanka poet, publishing in "Myojo" and "Subaru," the latter still going as a leading literary journal published by Shueisha. She met and was encouraged by Yosano Akiko when she was just seventeen. Her marriage to illustrator and manga artist Okamoto Ippei (he drew manga for the "Asahi Shimbun" and his work is in the collection of the British Museum) was an adventurous one, with a long trip overseas to Europe and the US. They had met in 1908 when she was on a trip with her father to Karuizawa in Nagano prefecture. In February 1911 she gave birth to her son Taro, who became one of Japan's greatest modern artists (his Tower of the Sun, erected for the 1970 Osaka Expo, still stands). The book of her letters to him is one of my favorite books, exploring, in a kindly and wise manner, the bond between mother and son.

Okamoto's writing career has two distinct periods. She published four books of tanka, the last in 1929. She deliberately put an end to this by titling the book *Waga Saishu Kashu* (*My Final Collection of Poems*), published by the great progressive house Kaizosha (their magazine, "Kaizo," published works by Margaret Sanger, Bertrand Russell, Boris Pilnyak, among many others; it was closed down by government order in 1944).

Okamoto was not a highly popular writer in her time, though her writing appeared in very respectable journals, such as "Bungakukai." The major work published there, in 1936, was her novella *Tsuru wa Yamiki* (*The Crane Falls Ill*) about the life and death of the novelist Akutagawa Ryunosuke. Akutagawa suffered from serious depression, as did Okamoto herself. The novella, whose publication was championed by Kawabata Yasunari, featured many literary figures as characters, albeit with their names changed. But it wasn't hard to discern who was who; and Tanizaki Junichiro, above all, was none too pleased by the portrait of himself and his actor sister-in-law in it. This novella brought her much notoriety and recognition in the last three years of her life.

Okamoto spent much time delving into the study of Buddhism,

particularly after finding herself drawn to the faith after the death of her second son and daughter in infancy, and considered herself a scholar of Buddhism as well as an author of fiction. Her relationship with Ippei had its steep ups and downs, but he was generally an open-minded partner, turning a half-blind eye to her extramarital relationships and even opening the doors of the home to one of her lovers. She was a feisty and self-assertive woman by her own admission and rarely did cooking or housework. When she admonished the maid once for not doing a thorough job, the maid said, "Well, then, madame, why don't you try your hand at it?" She apparently had no answer to this and burst into tears. Much of what we know of her personality and desires comes from Setouchi Jakuchu's detailed biography, *Kanoko Ryoran* (loosely, *Kanoko in All Her Glory*). It is a biography of one modern liberated Japanese woman written by another (Setouchi is also known for her liberated attitude toward love, and she shares with Okamoto a deep Buddhist faith, so much so that she became a nun). I read *Kanoko Ryoran* a few years ago. Okamoto's life reads like that of a Hollywood diva, though a diva she most certainly wasn't.

A stroke took her life in 1939 and for many years she was all but forgotten, until the postwar advocates of the women's liberation movement in Japan rediscovered her in the 1970s. Today she is an icon for Japanese feminists.

In 1962 Okamoto Taro sculpted a beautiful monument that stands on the bank of the Tama River in the precincts of the Tama Shrine. It is three hundred meters from his mother's childhood home. The monument is called "Pride" and these words are engraved in it: "I dedicate this Pride to the departed souls Ippei and Kanoko (signed) Taro."

With this monument and the cherry blossom trees along the banks of the Tama River in mind, I have chosen tanka on the theme of Japan's emblematic flower.

TANKA
OKAMOTO KANOKO

<u>In Front of the Station</u>
Cherry blossom petals are scattering
Gleaming in the noonday sun
On a bed of coal.

<u>By the Side of the Road</u>
The tires of an automobile have left
A cloud of thick dust rising
Below a cherry blossom tree.

<u>Utamaro Woodblock Print</u>
The small pale petals of the cherry blossom
On the courtesan's neck
Have fallen onto my bamboo-and-paper umbrella.

<u>Shining</u>
The rays of the sun that are shining meticulously
On each and every pine needle
Are shining equally on the cherry blossoms.

<u>Temple Garden</u>
The camellias lay rotting in the garden
In the grand old temple
While the cherry blossoms scatter
Throughout the branches of the magnolia.

<u>Twilight</u>
One large raven has returned
Without making a sound
To the mountain blanketed in cherry blossoms
Under a leaden sky.

SAGAWA CHIKA (1911-1936) was a poet whose life was cut short (at the age of twenty-four) by stomach cancer. Though she was unable to amass a large following for her poetry in her lifetime, she managed to make a reputation as a translator of writers such as James Joyce, Virginia Woolf, Aldous Huxley and Sherwood Anderson. She made a living as an English teacher. It is only in recent years that she has been rediscovered as one of the most original and exciting poetic voices in modern Japan.

Sagawa Chika is a penname, and the surname, Sagawa, is written with the characters for "left bank," namely the left bank of the Seine. In the year of her death Ito Sei, like Sagawa a native of Hokkaido, a poet and translator (his 1950 translation of *Lady Chatterley's Lover* sold 200,000 copies, but he was indicted with his publisher Oyama Hisajiro on obscenity charges), edited a collection of her poems and published them with Shorinsha. But it wasn't until 1983 that a comprehensive anthology of her writing saw the light of day. Many of her poems are permeated with an exquisite and deeply felt eroticism.

Sagawa lived her later years at Sakuragaoka in Setagaya ward, not far from where I lived in Tokyo. I include a relatively large selection of her poems here—some of which I did not read on the Youtube channel—because I believe her to be as great a poet in free verse as Yosano Akiko was in tanka.

THE INSECTS

SAGAWA CHIKA

The insects were reproducing fast, like electric current
Devouring every swelling on the Earth's crust.

The city night slept like a woman
Turning its gorgeous robes inside out.

I will now dry out my shell.
My scale-like skin is as cold as metal.

No one fathoms the secret that is layered
Over my profile.

A marked woman is spinning stolen expressions at will
While the night sends her into seventh heaven.

GLASS WINGS

SAGAWA CHIKA

The sun is caught between glass wings on the street corner

Smothering love

As it is passed with great care

From person to person.

The sky sits opposite my window

Darkening with every turn of the fan's blade.

Leaves fill the sky

Forming a single line above inclining roofs.

Trains creep over the swelling city streets

While sailors' neckbands describe circles

Among blue folds in the air.

Lines of people, all decked out for summer

Pass by, then collapse into a water bottle.

And the fruits of our mind pour down in joyful shadows.

A FRAGMENT

SAGAWA CHIKA

The blue officers are lined up
With their military caps made of cloud.
They are chopping off the heads of the night
From inside their infinite pits.
The sky and the trees are falling on top of each other
As if in the heat of battle.
An antenna swiftly intersects the space above them.
Are petals floating there as well?
It is noon and two suns have raced up the amphitheater.
It won't be long before the rusted red passions of summer
Slice our love in two.

The last two lines of "A Fragment" change the narrative from something epic (officers, battle, amphitheater) into the arch-personal. There is blinding light and abysmal dark in this poem that ends with love cut in two by passion's rusted blade.

BLACK AIR

SAGAWA CHIKA

In the distance twilight severs the sun's tongue.

Cities and towns in the underwater sky

Cease to laugh.

A shadow falls from every tree

To surround me where I am.

Forests and windowpanes turn pale

Like women. And the night

Has enveloped everything.

A bus is cutting across the park

Carrying a flame on it.

It's then that my passions dance through the town

Until every bit of sorrow has been driven away.

Though of only twelve lines and not fourteen, this poem strikes me as a perfect Japanese sonnet.

A FLOWER

SAGAWA CHIKA

Dreams are fruit that have been cut away.
Sepia pears have tumbled into the fields.
Parsley is blooming on a plate.
At times, leghorn chickens appear to have six toes.
And the moon comes out at the crack of an egg.

PHANTOM HOME

SAGAWA CHIKA

A chef grabs hold of a clear blue sky
Leaving four fingerprints
As blood oozes out of a chicken.
Even here the sun is collapsed on itself.
The warder of the sky has come again
And I watch the sunshine as it rushes away.
There's a house here deserted, without a soul.
It is surrounded by people's lingering dreams
Dreams that wither like flower petals.
By slow degrees death clings to my fingers
As it removes the husks of night one by one.
But that house never stays on the magnificent road
That leads to faraway recollections of a faraway world.

Another sonnet-like poem—gloomy and plaintive—that unites the world of food (chicken, husks) with the sky, the sun and a road that leads to the past.

THE DAY THE BELL TOLLS
SAGAWA CHIKA

All day long
I can hear the moaning of dead leaves
As they are trampled underfoot.
And, as it is with life's afternoon
The sound of the bell informs us
Of the hours that have faded away.
It whittles away at a tree's flesh
One cut at a time.
And by then
There is no time for anything anymore.

RIBBONS IN MAY

SAGAWA CHIKA

The air outside my window burst into laughter
And leaves blew in clusters
In the many-colored shadows of its tongue.
I've lost my ability to think.
Is someone there?
When I reached out into the dark
The only thing I could touch
Was the long hair of the wind.

Here Sagawa unites parts of a body (tongue, hair) and human actions (laughter, thinking, reaching) with the elements. Even the title relates an intimate human object with a season.

THE MOUNTAIN RANGE
SAGAWA CHIKA

The distant peaks are quivering like the wind.
The flowers in the orchard at the foot of the mountains
Have come out white as snow.
The face of the mountain has remained in winter
Unrolling every morning like silk.
I only wish to worship and to thank
This invisible thing that flows
Into my eyes with its sounds.
But no one is listening to me!
No one will forgive me!
Will the turtledove share my tears
And cry out an echo for me?
As the snow disappears
Rhododendrons and red lilies are bound to bloom
Forming green shadows in the valley.
The languid summer will conceal itself
Amid stinging nettles.
And gorgeous flames will describe a circle
In our heart.

TO SKIES FULL OF FLOWERS
SAGAWA CHIKA

Here is every person's eye.
Don't these words carry a white echo?
I'm going to take off my hat and stuff everything in
Just as the sky and the seas conceal untold petals.
And someday, blue fish and little rosy birds
Will pierce my head.
I don't think things that you lose
Ever come back.

MASAOKA SHIKI (1867-1902) was a poet, author, journalist, essayist, and one of the greatest literary reformers of the modern era. In many ways his theories, and the brilliant manner in which he illustrated them in his poetry, were ahead of his times in Europe as well as in Japan. His thousands of haiku and tanka form an immense photo gallery: You take in each one as you would clever and revealing photographs. As with all good haiku, despite the ambiguities and mysteries in them, the focus is ever sharp. Translations into European languages, including English, that produce a hazy, vague, wispy pseudo-Oriental impression to my mind miss the point. Masaoka Shiki's haiku are brilliantly clear and finely focused, concrete and often hyperrealistic to the point of mundanity.

He was born in Matsuyama, in Shikoku, and his hometown figures prominently in his work. As a young man he aspired to be a politician, a goal which in early-Meiji Japan was not such the absurd choice for a creative person as it might seem in that country today. He was a practicing and successful journalist, had a wide variety of intimate friends in the literary world, people of the stature of novelists Mori Ogai and Natsume Soseki (with whom he stayed in Matsuyama while ill), and Yosano Tekkan among them. He died in 1902 after years bedridden with tuberculosis, which he began suffering from when he was twenty-one. He served as a war correspondent in China during the Sino-Japanese War, but found his illness only worsening due to conditions in the field. He made his way via Kobe back to Matsuyama and moved into Natsume Soseki's home. His condition worsened to such an extent that by 1899 he could no longer sit for the pain, and could barely walk, venturing away from home only occasionally in a rickshaw. He said, "I want to be buried in a quiet temple"; and he lies in Tairyuji Temple in the inner Tokyo suburb of Tabata.

Aware, no doubt, of his impending death, he wrote of his wish for the future, of the "final state, the zero wish … the Buddha may have called it Nirvana…."

HAIKU
MASAOKA SHIKI

Autumn fly
The swatters are all full
Of holes

This is an intriguing image. The swatter has been used so much that holes have opened up in it. This indicates that the autumn fly's life may be saved thanks to the sacrifices made by its predecessors.

Shrill cicadas
Shriller than shrill cicadas
Is all

All of Shiki's haiku are hard to translate, but this is one of the hardest. The original is written entirely in katakana and reads:

tsukutsukuboshi
tsukutsukuboshi
bakarinari

The word that seemed to me to best characterize the incessant sound of the tsukutsukuboshi cicada is the mimetic "shrill." The last two words, "is all," have two meanings: all that I hear and all that there is.

Cockscombs
14, 15
It's hard to tell

There has been a controversy in high literary circles for many decades as to whether this is a haiku or not. It is so prosaic and simple that some critics dismiss it. But, if haiku are in essence visual definitions of things, then this eminently qualifies. The Japanese cockscomb, or *keito*, is a flower that resembles, with its many folds, the top half of a brain or the combs of chickens. When growing in a clump, it would definitely be hard to tell how many there were. So, this haiku works as a kind of visual definition, telling us that if you want to know what a cockscomb is like, it's a flower that can be hard to distinguish individuals in. Or … is it that the poet who is looking outside from his sickbed is experiencing, due to his illness, blurred vision?

A frog is floating
In a water jar
In the early summer rain

Where did all these cousins come from
In my hometown
The peach tree is flowering

The red light district
Just ten steps away …
And this autumn sky!

The white lines of the baseball diamond
Are enclosed
By thick tall weeds

Masaoka absolutely loved baseball and even wrote a textbook about the sport. His real given name was Noboru, and he went to the extent of writing it with the two Japanese characters *ya-kyu*, because *ya* can also be read *no*, and *kyu* is a "ball," or, in Japanese pronunciation, *bo-ru*, hence Nobo-ru. I love the sepia photograph of him taken in March 1890. Dressed in a baseball uniform he sits, looking pensively askance before a rural landscape—clearly a studio backdrop—holding a bat.

All my blank sheets of paper
Are taken by the wind
Of a summer storm

The sound of clippers cutting
Roses, in the air
On a perfect day in May

The snail is enticing
Rain clouds
With its antennae

This haiku employs one of the key elements seen in the genre, that of contrasting scale. We can see the snail's antennae, the sky and the whole space in between at once. Haiku often make you look elsewhere in order to see something central. In other words—and this can be said for much of Japanese aesthetics—things on the periphery of or quite a distance away from something may call attention to that thing much more vividly than the thing does itself. It is a kind of poetic entanglement.

Such emptiness!
A shooting star
Over the trace of fireworks

The hydrangeas
Pale blue in the rain
Bright blue under the moon

Again a kind of definition attached to a flower, this time of its varying colors in varying conditions.

The hydrangeas and the rain
Spray
A patch of crumbling wall

That old pond
And on it floats a cicada's shell
Upside down

Masaoka, it is known, was very critical of the great haiku poet Basho. Is this haiku, with its all too blatant reference to "that old pond," a comment on the old master? (Basho's haiku about a frog jumping into an old pond and making a splash is his most famous one.)

My hot water bottle spills out
Into the moonlight
On the old garden

The branches of two pine trees
Tug against each other
As autumn gives way to winter

When I peel my pear
Sweet droplets trickle
Against the blade

I read through
3000 haiku
Ate two persimmons

The contrast here is not in space but in time. Does this tell us how fast he can read this ultra-short form of poem … or how slowly he must eat because he is ill?

The tolling of the bell
Comes to me in a ring
On long nights

The double meaning of "ring" here is evident as he listens from his futon, unable to sleep in the dead of night.

A few stones
Are lying about where they fell
On the withered field

The path drops off
Just outside the front gate
Into a wintertime cluster of trees

He cannot see much further than the gate in this chilling winter scene.

I don't know how many times
I've asked people how deep
The snow is

A drop of dew fell on me
In my sickbed
Or so it seemed

Five daughters then finally a boy
And the first carp pennant
Is hoisted into the air!

I love this life-affirming haiku describing Children's Day (called "Boys' Day" up to 1948) on 5 May. It is still the custom in Japan to fly carp pennants in early May in celebration of the little boys in a family. Girls' Day is celebrated on 3 March with a display of traditional dolls.

Every day in my sickbed
Munching on rice cakes …
I'm in heaven!

The ambiguity of the last line is brought out by the word *higan*, which can either be taken literally to mean "I am already as good as dead" or "I am in a state of bliss" thanks, no doubt, to being able to stuff himself on rice cakes, a symbol of a new year … which he may or may not see. I've rendered it with the double-meaning "I'm in heaven."

KOBAYASHI ISSA (1763-1828) was one of the great haiku poets of the Edo period (1603-1867). The details of his life are well known. Born in Kashiwabara, in what is now Nagano prefecture, he lost his mother at age three, was severely abused by his stepmother, turfed out of the house and sent off to Edo (now Tokyo) at age fourteen. Though not a monk, he shaved his head—a practice of some teachers at the time—and took to wearing priestly robes.

He married for the first time at age fifty-two. Three children were born to him and his wife, Kiku. All three perished. A fourth child was born, but his wife died not long after the birth and the child, too, died as a toddler, probably as a result of violence or neglect at the hand of its nurse. He married again, a woman named Yuki, but divorced not long after the marriage. The Japanese phrase *sandome no shojiki* (it's the third time that counts) surely applied to his final marriage, to Yao. He was, by all accounts, deliriously happy with her. But a fire destroyed their house, and they came to live in a little storehouse that still stands today. Kobayashi Issa died at the age sixty-five, not long after the fire. Shortly after his death Yao gave birth to a baby daughter.

He traveled much around Japan during his lifetime, particularly with a mind to visiting sites of religious interest. In the literature he is described as having been struck a number of times with palsy or paralysis. What he most likely suffered was mild strokes, or mini-strokes, one of which apparently left him, for some months, hemiplegic.

His haiku, taken as a whole, create a wonderful canvas of Japanese customs and thought of his time. He is like a great photographer who records all of the wonders of Japanese life, and these landscapes and portraits strike us with an unfading intensity. The area around Kashiwabara is very beautiful, and one can only imagine how pristine and lovely its mountains and the nearby exquisite Lake Nojiri must have appeared in his time. I have made two trips there, in mid-summer and mid-winter, and sitting in his little storehouse-home in the stillness, I heard his voice, as I continue to hear it now, again and again.

HAIKU
KOBAYASHI ISSA

The little orphan swallow

Once again opens its mouth

In vain

I have translated *tori* (bird) as swallow. Issa illustrated this haiku with a haiga, or haiku drawing, of a swallow. Swallows, a migrating bird, figure much in his haiku. Also, the play on words with the verb "to swallow" seems to work here. Such plays on words are common in his haiku.

C'mon, play with me!

Orphan

Sparrow

The cows appeared

Out of the fog

Mooing and mooing and mooing

The repetition of the moo serves to portray the fog as deep and the number of cows, large. Or perhaps the cows were just happy to get into the clear.

I sleep on my back
With the midsummer clouds
Over my knees

The inference here is that the clouds are his blanket.

Side by side
Ice and lice
In my palm

My old dog
Leads the way
On a visit to the graves

I open a window
To send a butterfly off
Into the meadow

How beautiful!
The Milky Way from a hole
In my sliding rice-paper door

Again we see contrasting scales. Something as enormous as the Milky Way can fit into a hole in the rice paper ... or a farm worker, a mower, can been seen amid a vast storm of green ... or a frog's bottom can rival the summit of Mt. Fuji, as seen in the next two haiku.

The mower amidst the grass
On his horse, asleep
In a storm of green

A frog in the evening croaks
Lining up its bottom
With the top of Mt. Fuji

Skinny frog
Don't give up!
Issa is behind you

This is probably Issa's most famous haiku. It made into him a fighter on the side of
the weak and defenseless.

In a better world
I'd welcome more of you in my rice
Little fly

My little hut, my refuge
Luck be my companion
Toothless as I am

I'll be tossing in my sleep
So, move over
Cricket!

An empty stomach
Grumbling, thunder
Over the summer fields

Thanks to the shade
Below the cherry blossoms
Everyone knows everyone

Spring's hazy night
The liquor is flowing …
A waterfall moon

"Waterfall moon"—*taki no tsuki*—has to be one of the loveliest images in all his haiku. It is also suggestive of a generous flow of the good liquid.

Did you enjoy the festival
At Nikko
Cuckoo

The nightingale's morning
Voice was drowned out
By rain

The lark cries
Around the thicket
That conceals her chicks

In spite of the many feet
That have trampled it
The meadow flowers

Zenkoji Temple
Harvest time in Shinano
Buckwheat moon

Shinano is the old province name for what is now Nagano prefecture, where Zenkoji
Temple is located. This region was and still is famous for its soba, or buckwheat,
made into noodles.

In the Temple Hall
That silences men
A bee buzzes

I've got nobody to blame
For the chill of this journey
Save myself

Life's a journey, dew's
On the grass, whether you wish
To see it or not

I'll show you Matsushima
Then you're on your own
Little fleas

Among his many travels he made the pilgrimage to Matsushima, one of Japan's
most renowned beauty spots, in Miyagi prefecture, the fleas his only companion …
for a time.

A bird is building its nest
Unaware that the tree
Is marked for felling

A swallow shoots out
The nose
Of the Great Buddha

Big and small, great and insignificant, all shown at once in a snapshot of life and death, of this world and the next.

I sit crosslegged
A statue
Under a harvest moon

It is never easy to translate *hotoke*, which may be a Buddhist statue, a dead body or its spirit. Sitting crosslegged illustrates the Buddhist element.

Perfectly composed
The frog has its eyes
On the mountains

Even the spring butterfly
Finds itself inside the outhouse too
At Katsushika

Katsushika is a riverside suburb of Tokyo where one of his haiku masters, Sogan, lived. There is a contrast here of the beautiful and the ugly.

It grew somewhat chilly
When I learned how to write
The character for "Parent"

The awful fate of his children comes to mind here.

We tried to outstare each other
In the sweltering night
Me and that gargoyle

Oh well, is this to be
My final home
These six feet of snow

He wrote this at age fifty-one when he returned home to settle in Nagano. The opening words are very colloquial: *kore ga maa….* The last line—*yuki goshaku*—depicts a vision of his final resting place.

Even while strolling
Below the cherry blossoms
People are lecturing each other

Where do they come from
When the snow thaws
All these village children

The fields are on fire
The birds, too, seem to be saying ...
"Love when you can"

If you don't hear from me again
The offering of a flower
Is all the consideration I wish

BAISAO (1675-1763) was a Zen monk who spent his adult life moving from place to place in and around Kyoto peddling tea. The tea ceremony has its roots, among other things, in his dedication to the way of tea. Baisao's tea, his travels and his philosophy on life are one. At the end of his life he burnt the old baskets that had carried what he needed to make tea, thanking them for their service and sending them, in flames, to the sky.

A POEM WRITTEN BY CHANCE IN THE LUNAR JUNE
BAISAO

I sit calmly and alone
In the depths of the bamboo grove
Gathering what's left of my life and feeling
Apart from the mundane world.

The flowers that I have transplanted
To the back of my house
Are quietly displaying
Their colorful beauty.

I face the rocks
Looking out to my garden
And listen to voiceless voices.

I am at rest on the bank of the river
Where the sounds of the sutras
Reverberate in their recitation.

And when I amble around the pond
The purity of the lotus flowers' fragrance
Strikes me.

When visitors ask
"What is the secret essence of Zen
And how may I acquire it?"
I tell them that by doing my job
Of selling tea it should be clear

That the state of Zen
Is nothing more … or less.

TAKAMURA KOTARO (1883-1956) was a poet, painter and sculptor, and a leading intellectual force in the first half of the twentieth century. His marriage to the artist Naganuma Chieko is one of the most well-known love stories of modern Japan.

They first met in December 1911, when she visited his atelier, and had another encounter in September 1913. This led to their engagement and subsequent marriage in December 1914. She was a member of the feminist group Seitosha (The Bluestocking Society) from its inception and an ardent advocate of women's rights. In fact, her illustration appeared on the cover of the very first issue of their magazine, "Seito," in 1911. Chieko and Kotaro were famous for having an open marriage. But in 1931 she was diagnosed with schizophrenia and tuberculosis. She spent her later years in and out of hospital, creating a large body of paper art from her bed. She passed away in 1938 at the age of fifty-two.

In 1903 Takamura encountered the work of Rodin, writing in his diary of the deep and unforgettable impression it made on him. A year later a photograph of "The Thinker" in the February issue of the art magazine "Studio" solidified this impression and made Rodin the inspiration of his own sculpture from then on.

Takamura sailed out of Yokohama harbor on 3 February 1906 bound for the US. He enrolled in the night school of New York's National Academy of Design, which, at the time, was occupying the American Fine Arts Society building at 215 West 57th St. In June 1907 he went to Britain where he became a student at Frank Brangwyn's School of Art. Brangwyn was already by then a distinguished Welsh painter and designer who had opened his own art school in 1904 in a mews off Stratford Road in Kensington. It was through the school that Takamura met the potter Bernard Leach, with whom he became lifelong friends. In November of that year he visited Rodin's atelier in France.

Takamura again left London for Paris in June 1908 and opened a small atelier of his own in Montparnasse. He stayed there until

March of the following year when he traveled around Italy and, after stopping off for the last time in Paris and London, boarded a ship and returned to Japan, arriving in Kobe on 30 June 1909.

Takamura was known for decades in Japan as the great Westernized Japanese, a free thinker and critic who deepened his compatriots' interest in many nonJapanese artists and writers, such as Rodin, Van Gogh and Whitman. But as Japan's artistic freedom and democratic institutions were trampled into the ground by the stamp of military boots in the 1930s Takamura threw himself gung-ho into the camp of aggression and invasion. His influence among Japan's intellectuals was so great that many of them who had wavered felt that if Takamura Kotaro supported the government then their imperialist ambitions and aggressive military actions must be just. During the war Takamura wrote many formulaic patriotic poems.

After the war, however, he came to regret his actions. Miyazawa Kenji's brother Seiroku invited him to come and live in Hanamaki, in Iwate prefecture. (Kenji had visited Takamura's atelier, and the latter was an early admirer of his poetry.) On the night of 15 May 1945, while the war was still raging and American B-29 superfortresses were carpetbombing Japanese cities, Takamura left Ueno Station in Tokyo for Hanamaki. On 10 August, just five days before the Japanese surrender, Hanamaki, a town without any military significance, was bombed, and the Miyazawa home was severely damaged. (Fortunately, Seiroku had taken the precaution of removing his brother's manuscripts to a safe place.) On 17 October Takamura moved into a little hut on the outskirts of the town and, cultivating his own vegetables, lived there. It was a kind of penance.

He died in the early morning of 2 April 1956 at an atelier that he had established in Tokyo's Nakano ward.

As can be seen from the second poem here, "The Country of Netsuke," he may have been a chauvinist, but he was an astute observer of, not an apologist for, the national character of his people.

INNOCENCE
TAKAMURA KOTARO

Chieko tells me that Tokyo has no sky.
"I'm dying to see a real sky," she says.
I look up to the sky with alarm.
But there it is, a part of me
The old blue sky
Amidst the green leaves of a cherry blossom tree.
The shadings in the dull haze on the horizon
Come from the pale pink morning damp.
Chieko speaks with her eyes far away …
"The blue sky that rises every day
Over the top of Mt. Atatara
Is the only real sky."
Only the innocent speak that way
About the sky.

"Innocence" was written in May 1928. Mt. Atatara is in Fukushima prefecture, near the town of Nihonmatsu, where Chieko was born.

THE COUNTRY OF NETSUKE
TAKAMURA KOTARO

With angular cheekbones and thick lips
With eyes like triangles and a face like a netsuke
Carved by Grand Master Sangoro
A look that is vacant and vacuous
As if the soul had been extracted
Lacking in self-knowledge
Always fussing over trivialities
A vain fop who does not value life
Shrimpy, implacable, smug
Looks like a monkey
Looks like a fox
Looks like a flying squirrel
Looks like a pint-size goby
Looks like a ricefish
Looks like a gargoyle
Looks like the chip off a teacup …
The Japanese!

"The Country of Netsuke" was written in December 1910, after Takamura's return from his more than three years overseas. Netsuke are small sculpted objects, either made for ornamental purposes or used by men to attach something—a pipe, a tobacco pouch or box—to the obi of a kimono. Actually, there is no such grand master of netsuke by the name of Sangoro, and it's not known how Takamura came by it. In a 1929 edition of the poem he conspicuously changed the name to a real master of this Edo period art form, namely Shuzan. But in later editions he changed it back because, as he said, "I like the way it sounds."

MIYAZAWA KENJI (1896-1933) was a poet and author from Hanamaki in Iwate prefecture. I have spent more than fifty years studying and translating him and his work and would refer the reader to my collection of his stories, *Night on the Milky Way Train*, published by Balestier Press, and of his poems, published by Bloodaxe Books, *Strong in the Rain*, the title having been taken from Kenji's most famous poem (and Japan's most memorized poem) below.

He was a poet of immense empathy for all people who suffer misery or pain, and he believed that his own joy could only come from the joys of others. He was decades ahead of his time in his ideas of social design, writing about climate change, ecology and cruelty to animals (he was a vegetarian from age twenty-one and one of the first to assail those who harmed or killed animals) when the preoccupations of his compatriots were overwhelmingly centered on Japanese national pride and racial superiority.

When he died of tuberculosis on 21 September 1933 his published legacy was only two books, the publication of which he had paid for himself. It wasn't until after the war that his reputation began to grow significantly, and he is today considered by many to be Japan's greatest twentieth-century poet.

POLITICIANS

MIYAZAWA KENJI

They're just a bunch of scaremongers
Raising alarm wherever they can
And drinking their fill all the while
   fern fronds and clouds
      the world is that cold and dark
And before they know it
These fellows
Rot all on their own
Are washed away by the rains all on their own
Leaving nothing but silent blue ferns
Then some lucid geologist will come along and put this on record

As the Carboniferous Age of man

His poetry often contains sudden juxtapositions and non sequiturs referring to natural phenomena, such as those in lines four and five, as well as snippets of conversations. As he tells us in "Politicians," we are living in the "Carboniferous Age of man." The adjective modifying "geologist" is *tomei na*, which literally translates as "transparent." But it can also mean "earnest," as when it modifies "scholar" or similar title. So I have chosen "lucid" to encompass both meanings, also because it is etymologically related to the Latin word for "light" … and Miyazawa Kenji's descriptions of light in his works are the most beautiful in the Japanese language. He was, in a word, "the poet of light."

STRONG IN THE RAIN

MIYAZAWA KENJI

Strong in the rain
Strong in the wind
Strong against the summer heat and snow
He is healthy and robust
Free from desire
He never loses his temper
Nor the quiet smile on his lips
He eats four *go* of unpolished rice
Miso and a few vegetables a day
He does not consider himself
In whatever occurs
His understanding
Comes from observation and experience
And he never loses sight of things
He lives in a little thatched-roof hut
In a field in the shadows of a pine tree grove
If there is a sick child in the east
He goes there to nurse the child
If there's a tired mother in the west
He goes to her and carries her sheaves
If someone is near death in the south
He goes and says, "Don't be afraid"
If there are strife and lawsuits in the north
He demands that the people put an end to their pettiness

He weeps at the time of drought
He plods about at a loss during the cold summer
Everybody calls him Blockhead
No one sings his praises
Or takes him to heart

That is the kind of person
I want to be

A *go* of rice is approximately 150 grams when dry but makes about 350 grams of cooked rice. Unpolished rice, or *genmai*, is not generally eaten in Japan today but before the war it was a staple, particularly of the less well to do. Miyazawa, who was the oldest son in a very wealthy family, is here identifying with the disadvantaged. He repeats "goes" to show that a person's character is judged by their actions, not their words or the recognition they get. As a trained scientist he emphasizes that a person's understanding of human nature and the world comes from observation and experience. Though he was a devout Buddhist from the time he was a teenager, he believed that true faith came not from blind belief but rather from learning the truths of the natural world.

THE FUN PARK
ROGER PULVERS

for Shibata Motoyuki

Once you enter
You can hardly believe your eyes.
The lights are blinding
Drawing you to them
Here, there … everywhere.

Then there's the lush pool
Deep as an ocean
Begging you to take the plunge.
And when you get out of your depth
An adult is always on hand
To lift you from the water
High into the air.

And the slide …
It's a mile long!
No matter how fast you fly
The end remains out of sight.
Even when you reach it
You're free to go back
To make the trip again and again
Countless trips
Countless times.

Look toward the entrance to the park.
The lights are all ablaze.

But then the day begins to pass, slowly at first.
You get your cotton candy.
It's flat and sweet against your tongue.
Your hot dog is smothered in relish.
Even the dry end of the bun
Tastes a bit like heaven.

But before you know it
It's closing time.
You find yourself walking in the dark.
The old adults by the pool are long gone.

You are free to look back just one more time.
The lights are no longer blinding
And everything there is exactly the same as when you came in:
The deep pool … the long slide
The hot dog stand
And the funny cotton candy man.

Index of Poems